Developing Teachers as Leaders

Educational Leadership and Leaders in Contexts

Founding Editors

Tony Townsend (*Florida Atlantic University, Boca Raton, Florida, USA*)
Ira Bogotch (*Florida Atlantic University, Boca Raton, Florida, USA*)

VOLUME 7

The titles published in this series are listed at *brill.com/ellc*

Developing Teachers as Leaders

A Reflective Writing Approach

By

Phil Quirke, Joy Kreeft Peyton, Jill Burton,
Carla Reichmann and Latricia Trites

BRILL
SENSE

LEIDEN | BOSTON

Cover illustration: *Abstract Sunset*, original work by Latricia Trites

All chapters in this book have undergone peer review.

The Library of Congress Cataloging-in-Publication Data is available online at http://catalog.loc.gov

Typeface for the Latin, Greek, and Cyrillic scripts: "Brill". See and download: brill.com/brill-typeface.

ISSN 2666-7746
ISBN 978-90-04-44914-5 (paperback)
ISBN 978-90-04-44915-2 (hardback)
ISBN 978-90-04-44916-9 (e-book)

Copyright 2021 by Koninklijke Brill NV, Leiden, The Netherlands.
Koninklijke Brill NV incorporates the imprints Brill, Brill Hes & De Graaf, Brill Nijhoff, Brill Rodopi, Brill Sense, Hotei Publishing, mentis Verlag, Verlag Ferdinand Schöningh and Wilhelm Fink Verlag.
All rights reserved. No part of this publication may be reproduced, translated, stored in a retrieval system, or transmitted in any form or by any means, electronic, mechanical, photocopying, recording or otherwise, without prior written permission from the publisher. Requests for re-use and/or translations must be addressed to Koninklijke Brill NV via brill.com or copyright.com.

This book is printed on acid-free paper and produced in a sustainable manner.

Contents

Acknowledgment VII
List of Figures and Tables VIII

1 **Reflective Writing and Its Potential for Developing Teacher Leaders** 1
 Phil Quirke, Joy Kreeft Peyton, Jill Burton, Carla Reichmann and Latricia Trites
 1 Importance of Reflective Writing in Learning, Teaching, and Leadership Development 2
 2 Forms of Reflective Writing 4
 3 Research on Reflective Writing 5
 4 Developing Depth in Reflective Writing 6
 5 Inquiry in Reflective Writing 8
 6 Reflective Writing in Teacher Leadership Development 9
 7 Chapters in This Book 10

2 **An Approach to Using Reflective Writing to Develop Teacher Leaders: DREAM Management** 18
 Phil Quirke
 1 Theoretical Structure of the Course 19
 2 Forms of Reflective Writing in Teacher Leader Development 22
 3 Participation Patterns in Reflective Writing for Teacher Leader Development 25
 4 Recruit 26
 5 Developing Depth in Reflective Writing for Teacher Leadership Development 29
 6 Increasing Depth of Reflection through Asking Why 38
 7 Conclusion 40

3 **Mentoring Reflection: Teaching Pre-Service Teachers to Ask Why** 48
 Latricia Trites
 1 Pre-Service Teacher Disconnect 50
 2 Limited Perspective of Cooperating Teacher/Mentors 51
 3 Explicit Instruction on Reflection 52
 4 Personal Reflection: A Local Model 54
 5 Next Steps for Mentoring Reflection 59
 6 Conclusion 62

4 Co-Leadership through Dialogue and Reflective Writing in the Teaching Practicum   65
    Carla Reichmann
    1 Core Concepts   67
    2 The Practicum: Macro and Microcontexts   69
    3 The Cooperating Teacher and University Supervisor Relationship   70
    4 Co-Leadership in the Practicum   72
    5 Reflections in Flux   79

5 Visions and Realities: Doctoral Perspectives on Practice and Leadership   84
    Jill Burton
    1 The Doctoral Environment   85
    2 Doctoral Methodologies   89
    3 Reflections   93
    4 Proflections   99

6 Patterns of Participation in Reflective Writing and Their Implications for Teacher Leadership Development   104
    Joy Kreeft Peyton and Phil Quirke
    1 Documenting Patterns of Participation in and Outcomes of Reflective Writing of Current and Prospective Teachers and Teacher Leaders   105
    2 Participation Patterns   105
    3 Participation Patterns and Outcomes of Teachers Developing as Leaders   111
    4 Implications for Teacher Leadership Development   117

7 Reflective Writing to Develop Teacher Leaders: Where to Go from Here   121
    Phil Quirke, Joy Kreeft Peyton, Jill Burton, Carla Reichmann and Latricia Trites
    1 Reflections on Developing Teachers as Leaders   121
    2 The Role of Reflective Writing in Leadership Development   122
    3 Reflecting on the Chapters in This Book: Raising Questions   124
    4 Implications for Written Reflective Inquiry in Teacher Leadership Education   127
    5 Types of Leadership   128
    6 Next Steps for the Authors of This Book   130
    7 Reflective Writing and Teachers as Leaders – Next Steps for Us and the Field   133

Index   137

Acknowledgment

All royalties from this book are donated to the Instituto dos Cegos da Paraiba Adalgisa Cunha (ICPAC), a school in João Pessoa, Paraíba, Brazil, that serves the low vision and blind community in the area. For years, the Institute has collaborated as a supervised internship site for various teacher education university programs, providing inspiring field work experiences such as those described in Chapter 4 by Carla Reichmann.

Brill is proud to support this important cause and match the donation to the Instituto dos Cegos da Paraiba Adalgisa Cunha (ICPAC). Please find out more about ICPAC here: http://icpac.com.br

Figures and Tables

Figures

2.1 Model of teacher knowledge development (from Quirke, 2009). 20
3.1 Mentoring reflection cycle. 61

Tables

1.1 Patterns in reflective writing (adapted from Gusky, 2000). 5
1.2 A reflective writing typology (adapted from Burton, 2005, 2009). 7
3.1 Years of experience as a cooperating teacher. 56
3.2 University supervisor experiences. 57
5.1 Cultural and educational backgrounds of students. 86
5.2 Professional experience and goals. 86
5.3 Research foci. 87
5.4 Research methodologies. 87
5.5 Reflective writing methodology. 89

CHAPTER 1

Reflective Writing and Its Potential for Developing Teacher Leaders

Phil Quirke, Joy Kreeft Peyton, Jill Burton, Carla Reichmann and Latricia Trites

This book is about using reflective writing to develop teachers as leaders, and focuses primarily on reflective writing and guiding teachers to recognise their leadership strengths. While recognizing the differences between management planning, organizing, and staffing and leadership visioning, directing, motivating, and inspiring, research has clearly demonstrated that leadership and management are complementary, with effective leadership requiring management skills and effective management needing leadership qualities (Bush, 2011; Fiedler & Garcia, 1987; Kotter, 1990; Marques & Dhiman, 2017). The metaphor of leadership as heart and management as head is an apt one, since one cannot survive without the other. The metaphor links neatly to the reflective approach taken throughout this book, where the development of teachers as leaders focuses on accentuating their pedagogical skills using hearts and heads in all of the scenarios described. Therefore, the book does not provide a detailed description of different leadership theories, although it does give readers references to pursue further those approaches that interest them.

Reflective writing can play a critical role in the development of teachers as leaders. This book examines the importance of reflective writing in how teachers, through choice or circumstance, can learn and function as leaders throughout their careers, whether they are situated in the classroom or an office. The chapters explore leadership considerations in a range of teaching contexts – cross-site, regional, national, and global. Each chapter raises diverse issues for teachers who find themselves functioning as leaders.

This chapter considers the forms that reflective writing can take, research on reflective writing and teacher development, and ways to develop depth in reflective writing. It reviews the theories behind reflective writing and reflective inquiry, focusing on the power of questions and their use in creating ever-deeper levels of reflection in the growth and development of educators as teachers, tutors, mentors, coaches, program managers, and teacher educators in the arena of educational leadership, areas that are underrepresented in the current literature.

1 Importance of Reflective Writing in Learning, Teaching, and Leadership Development

Teachers, and the act of teaching, are understood to be critical to students' success (Fullan, 1993). For example, Hargreaves and Fullan (2012), in a review of current practices of teaching and school leadership, claim that

> never before have teachers, teaching, and the future of teaching had such elevated importance. There is widespread agreement now that of all the factors inside the school that affect children's learning and achievement, the most important is the teacher – not standards, assessments, resources, or even the school's leadership, but the quality of the teacher. (p. xii)

Hargreaves and Fullan also argue that teachers need to exercise professional knowledge and know how to use professional resources – to be prepared to "teach like a pro", with a strong set of standards to meet "a personal commitment to rigorous training, continuous learning, collegial feedback, respect for evidence, responsiveness to parents, striving for excellence, and going far beyond the requirements of any written contract" (p. xiv).

At the same time, many teachers work in isolation, without collaboration or support from other teachers or school leaders and essentially are left to make hard decisions about teaching approaches and student achievement alone. Educational managers and school and district leaders may have become out of touch with the core teaching values of effective educational leadership at all levels, including, crucially, those at the classroom level, and so not be able to support teachers as adequately as they might. Teachers also often feel overloaded and pulled in many different directions. They are criticized from many quarters if they make one wrong move, in a challenging context of blame and shame. Teachers' contacts with new ideas, possibilities for effective participation in change processes, and opportunities to become acknowledged leaders in their areas of expertise are often severely limited because of this culture of isolation and blame. Teachers in reality are leaders, every day in their own classrooms, and many also have specialist expertise. Most experienced teachers regularly perform coaching and mentoring roles, mostly informally, without which educational institutions could not function effectively. Often it is those outside the classroom who are conventionally regarded as the drivers of reform and innovation, certainly in the wider community, because teachers are often too busy, or demoralized, to speak up. A lack of trust and respect between teachers and administrators is common.

These experiences of teachers and misperceptions of them have been reported, observed, and documented for many years (e.g., Fullan, 1993; Lortie, 2002; Pomson, 2005; Schlichte, Yessel, & Marbler, 2005) and continue in more recent scholarly publications (e.g., Farrell, 2013, 2018; Hargreaves & Fullan, 2012) and teacher testimonials; see, for example, a testimonial by teacher Simone Ryals, who noted online: "We must hate teachers. I've won awards, my kids thrive. But thanks to crazy tests, I'm being shamed" (2014).

Reflective practice, and specifically reflective writing, are approaches to teacher support and development that seek to address and rectify these experiences by allowing prospective and practicing teachers as teacher leaders to process current and newly learned practices in a deliberate, thoughtful, and focused fashion (e.g., Bolton, 2018; Chacón, 2018; Moon, 2004, 2006; Peyton, 2009; Sabah & Rashtchi, 2016; Schön, 1987; Wallace, 1991; Zeichner & Liston, 1996), within a safe, supportive, and interactive setting (Bailey, Curtis, & Nunan, 1998; Burton & Carroll, 2001; Farrell, 2007, 2013; Gallup-Rodríguez & McKay, 2010; Noffke & Brennan, 2005; Orem, 2001; Watanabe, 2016) that often takes the form of a community of practice (Burton 2013; Murphy & Sato, 2005; Singer-Gabella, 2012; Wenger, 1998; Wenger, McDermott, & Snyder, 2002). As we can see above, there are numerous discussions of these opportunities and their benefits and challenges.

There are many reasons to use reflective writing in education generally, and in teacher leadership development specifically. Most can be included under eight broadly stated goals. Reflective writing allows all educators to do the following:

1. Examine and reflect on their own knowledge, practice, experiences, and development, in a process of practical reasoning that emerges and changes over time, often in collaboration with others.
2. Clarify positions on critical issues in teaching, learning, and leadership.
3. Allow for evolving philosophies of teaching, learning, and leadership.
4. Express and question beliefs about teaching, learning, and leadership.
5. Develop content knowledge, language ability, teaching expertise, understanding of students, and awareness of educational leadership approaches.
6. Develop confidence in the ability to teach, mentor, manage, and lead effectively.
7. Understand other teachers and support them as they develop their own professional practice and grow as leaders.
8. Document patterns of classroom practice and change in classroom practice and schools; beliefs about teaching, learning, and leadership in the

teaching and learning endeavor; and confidence in the ability to teach and lead effectively.

Readers will see descriptions and examples of all these thought processes and practices, viewed from a number of different perspectives and in a range of contexts, in the chapters in this book.

2 Forms of Reflective Writing

Reflective writing can take many forms that involve personal (individual) and collaborative/interactive writing, in which teachers record and reflect on their experiences. Personal writing may include, among others, the following forms (see Quirke, 2018, for descriptions):
- Reflective teaching philosophy portfolios;
- Reader response journals on assigned readings;
- Classroom teaching journals;
- Personal development diaries;
- Autobiographies and memoirs for critical reflection;
- Analysis or case studies of critical incidents;
- Narratives.

Interactive writing between two or more people can take any of the following forms:
- *Guided reflective journals* – Teachers are asked to respond to guiding questions, the journal partner responds, and an ongoing conversation ensues.
- *Dialogue journals* – Prospective or practicing teachers write to each other or with an instructional leader or another teacher, with or without guiding questions (Peyton, 2000a, 2000b).
- *Small-group journals* – A group writing together can have a number of different configurations and can include classroom practitioners and leaders, administrators, professional developers, researchers, and others.
- *Online discussions* (e.g., online forums in class management systems such as Blackboard™ or Canvas, study circles, local and international writing communities) – These discussions can stand alone or be conducted in preparation for or as follow-up to face-to-face sessions.

All of these forms may be informal or formal, depending on their purpose (e.g., professional in-service networks, graduate coursework, and doctoral research). The chapters in this book describe a range of different forms of reflective writing that the authors, and the teachers and learners with whom they have worked, have used to promote reflection, growth, and leadership development.

3. Research on Reflective Writing

A helpful approach to considering the impact of reflective writing on developing teacher leaders is to investigate the forms that reflective writing can take, the types and forms of development that can occur in the writers, and outcomes of the reflective writing process. To provide a structure for a review of this research, we have adapted Guskey's framework (2000) for evaluating the outcomes of participation in professional development. The framework includes five categories: participant reactions, participant learning, participant use of new knowledge and skills, organization change and support, and student learning. We have added participation patterns as an additional category (see Table 1.1). Chapter 6 describes the ways that reflective writing can be reviewed for these patterns and outcomes and gives examples of writing from this review and analysis.

TABLE 1.1 Patterns in reflective writing (adapted from Gusky, 2000)

Participation patterns	Who participates? How much? In what ways?
Participant reactions	What do they think about the opportunity and their participation? Was the time well spent? Will it be useful to them in their work?
Participant learning	What knowledge and skills did participants acquire?
Participant use of new knowledge and skills	What changes took place in teaching as a result of participation and use of new knowledge and skills?
Organization change and support	What changed in participants' programs and schools as a result of the writing and reflection?
Student learning	What was the impact on students? How did teacher learning affect student performance or achievement?

An example of research on *participation patterns* can be found in Romero (2009), based on the work of Freire (1970) and the research of Smyth (1989, 1992). In her study of teachers writing with her, their mentor in an ongoing teacher education program, Romero found that over time, the teachers moved from describing, to informing, to confronting, to reconstructing, a process in which they developed their professional identities and demonstrated growth in themselves as teachers and potential leaders.

Participant reactions have been investigated using surveys of participants about their writing and reflection (Quirke, 2001), feedback forms at different stages of the reflective writing process or course, and closed- or open-ended questions or prompts answered in a journal or blog.

Participant learning has been investigated through interviews with participants, discourse analysis of their writing (Barnard & Burns, 2012; Burns & Burton, 2008), and narratives documenting linguistic evidence of change (Clandinin & Connelly, 2000). Examples of this research include the use of systemic functional grammar (Halliday, 1994) by Martin and Rose (2003) to explore how teachers write about and, over time, change their views about language and their use of language; the language used and learned by their students; their own learning processes (Reichmann, 2013); critical influences on their learning; their views of their jobs and their performance in their jobs; and their views of themselves as current or potential leaders and managers. Another example of investigating participant learning is lexico-grammatical evidence and critical discourse perspectives studied by Fairclough (1992).

Participants' use of new knowledge and skills has been examined using structured and open-ended questions in written interactions between practicing teachers and teacher educators and through review of and reflection on teacher lesson plans and classroom practices (Trites, Sroda, & Tseng, 2009).

Other research methods used include observing and documenting teacher behavior in classes and instructional foci in schools after teachers have participated in journal writing (*organization change and support*) and analyzing changes in student writing after participating in journal writing (*student learning*). Trites and Tseng (2009), as well as Albanese et al. (2009) and Wu, Martin, and Herbert (2008), discuss the importance of written reflection in collaboration and co-teaching, which can lead to effective mentoring practices to improve current and future teaching practices of pre-service and in-service teachers.

4   Developing Depth in Reflective Writing

Reflective writing can be used in a number of ways with current and prospective teachers as leaders through supporting the development of deeper perspectives, knowledge, and skills. One approach is a Reflective Writing Typology, developed by Burton (2005, 2009; shown in Table 1.2). The writing is presented as a series of steps that move writers from simple description of what happened in the classroom, a meeting, or a leadership event to deeper and more profound theorizing over time that encourages examination of beliefs about language, learning, pedagogy, psychology, and ways to work effectively with and lead others.

TABLE 1.2   A reflective writing typology (adapted from Burton, 2005, 2009)

Type	Answering questions	Comments
1	What happens/happened?	Recording, expressing, "getting the story down"
2	How does/did it happen?	Commenting on, attempting to explain: e.g., by adding more detail or approaching the Type 1 story from another perspective or question
3	Why does/did it happen? What does this mean outside the immediate context of action?	Theorizing on the story and reflection in Types 1 & 2, linking them to personal theories; e.g., of language, learning, and teaching
4	Are the earlier reflections credible/reasonable? Why? Why not? What do they mean now?	A subsequent written reflection in a developing sequence of reflective writing, in which writers continue to question and maybe involve others
5	Are the earlier reflections still credible/reasonable? Why? Why not? What do they mean now in the light of subsequent experience?	After longer intervals, writers use the developing spiral of reflection (which may include other writers: e.g., as part of an interactive journal) to re-examine initial theorizing in light of intervening events that may have changed their perspectives

It is a deceptively simple framework that produces powerful reflection and can be a springboard to more complex reflective writing over time, or it can be used as an analytic framework to review written texts and consider the levels and kinds of reflection that they contain.

Another approach to promoting and studying participant learning over time was developed by Spencer (2009), using a Phenomenological Framework based on the works of Gadamer (1976), Heidegger (1982), Husserl (1931), Merleau-Ponty (1964), Ricoeur (1981), and van Manen (2007). In this framework, the teacher

- Starts with an experience;
- Records the experience in writing;
- Creates a narrative about the experience within a larger educational, social, political, and national context;
- Identifies overarching themes that arise;
- Processes those themes by investigating a rich set of resources, with input from personal reflection, diaries and journals, literature on the themes, and other sources;
- Reflects on what has been learned;
- Looks back at the experience, now with a new lens, and considers possible new ways to move forward.

5 Inquiry in Reflective Writing

The use of inquiry to promote writer reflection has emerged as a practice in teacher education (e.g., Appreciative Inquiry; see He, 2013). An inquiry approach that we have taken, and that resonates throughout this book, is a "Why" approach to reflection that opens new ways of looking at experience and growth. The Why that we ask in this approach is what we call a "True Why", because it does not involve or imply judgment. When we ask "Why?" there is no implication that something else should have been done. With a "True Why", the teacher as leader, educator, or manager is asking a genuine question about their own or another person's actions, motivations, thoughts, and reflections on what has been done, what has not been done, or what has been done in a specific way. The questioner really wants and needs to know and wants the reflection to be profound and provide an avenue for change, for new paths to explore and pursue. This approach to questions and reflection is easier said than done, so in the chapters of this book, we explore ways that experienced teacher educators and current and emerging leaders can use the "True Why" to create opportunities for deeper reflection about personal theories on management, leadership, teaching, and learning, and how they combine.

These approaches to implementing and studying reflective writing build on and expand our earlier research, reported in *Reflective Writing: A Way to Lifelong Teacher Learning* (Burton, Quirke, Reichmann, & Peyton, 2009). That book includes contributions from a wide range of authors focused on uses of reflective writing in their instructional practice. Here, we expand our focus to explore the power of questions and ways that experienced and emerging teacher leaders and teacher educators can use questions effectively to promote deeper reflection and leadership development using different levels of Why questions.

All of the chapters theorize from practice and draw extensively on how self-directed teacher learners use written reflection to learn and develop further and become teacher leaders. The book represents our attempt, as experienced reflective practitioners, to provide a reflective writing framework to enhance teacher leadership development that can be used in different contexts, employing reflective writing and questioning as a central construct for delving deeply and uniquely into teaching and leadership practice, whether it involves teachers, teacher educators, mentors, coaches, managers, administrators, or other types of leaders. (See the discussions of coaches and managers as they emerge throughout the book and are discussed in Chapter 7.)

The reflective writing approach described here focuses on self-development, which includes the critical concept of identity (Olsen, 2010, 2012). The approach does not involve promoting any specific leadership or identity theory (although leadership theories to explore are suggested in Chapter 2) but instead, opens the door for teachers as individuals to examine and learn about their professional roles and potential as leaders from their education contexts. Through systematic reflection, they learn to investigate and to explain how to function professionally and take responsibility for their learning and growth, which is the power of reflective writing approaches such as this. Because the individuals involved are supported in taking responsibility for their own growth and renewal, the critical processes involved in reflective writing are constructive, encouraging further questioning and innovation. Participants are encouraged to expand their thinking critically and not to restrict their sense of what they can achieve in the classroom, their department, the school, or the institution.

6   Reflective Writing in Teacher Leadership Development

Reflective writing is a powerful tool in teacher leadership development, as its use in education management and leadership courses can give participants the opportunity to explore contexts in which they take professional roles as mentors, coaches, administrative support leaders, and curriculum or professional development leaders. Teachers can be given opportunities to examine educational leadership theories, the essential qualities of educational leaders, the key components of leadership, and the applicability of these to their own approaches to professional growth.

Effective education for teacher learners involves them in experiencing leadership roles, such as how to create and maintain a classroom environment that is conducive to collaborative learning with and for students. Similarly, teacher leadership involves the ability to create and maintain an environment in a school, district, state, or other entity that enhances socially constructed collaborative learning (Grossman, 1990; Hall & Simeral, 2017; Rosen, 1996; Vygotsky, 1978; Wink & Putney, 2002) with all staff, faculty, and students. Classroom leadership focuses on 'observables' in teaching – space, time, learning and teaching activities, communication, interaction, atmosphere, and artifacts. Effective education leadership also focuses on 'observables' – in teaching, student performance, professional development, institutional quality, human resources, facilities, and the financial health of the institution. Classroom leadership also highlights 'unobservables' – individual affective, social, and psychological factors; cognitive domain factors; group factors; and wider social, cultural, and other influences (Atkinson & Claxton, 2003). More widely, effective educational leadership highlights these 'unobservables' and consciously builds them into the vision, strategies, and day-to-day operational management of the classroom, department, school, or institution (Marques & Dhiman, 2017). By using the link between effective classroom leadership and broader educational leadership, reflective writing allows teachers to explore new theories from a different discipline and discern which of these apply best to their context, professional identity, and organizational style.

Reflective writing, individually and within and across teams, can promote leadership development as participants map their existing skills and abilities onto their new or prospective roles and explore together how best to apply leadership theories to their roles and approaches. The literature on reflective practice and reflective writing, reviewed above, provides a rich basis for the use of reflective writing in guiding participants to build on their existing knowledge and continue to grow as professionals and leaders.

7 Chapters in This Book

The chapters in this book explore the power of reflection in leadership development through the voices and lives of teachers, researchers, teacher leaders (as mentors, coaches, and administrators, who may also teach), and teacher educators, and the processes that we, as authors and leaders, have used to examine them. In particular, we document reflective writing experiences and the ways that these individuals and groups, and we as their colleagues, have grown through them. We reflect on how individual voices have an impact on leadership development through, for example, the use of reflective writing in teacher leadership courses.

Chapter 2, "An Approach to Using Reflective Writing to Develop Teacher Leaders: DREAM Management", by Phil Quirke, describes one method of educational leadership training that implements the DREAM management approach (Quirke, 2011; Quirke & Allison, 2008, 2010) to educational leadership and how the approach has been implemented in leadership development courses in the United Arab Emirates (UAE). It explains the theoretical framework for and components of the approach and how its principles can be applied to contexts in which teacher leaders are poised to take professional roles outside of their own classrooms.

The chapter explicitly links the approaches to reflective writing described in Chapter 1 and current management and leadership theories. It discusses how concepts such as the policy contexts in which teachers work, the opportunities for teachers to move into management and leadership roles (within and outside the classroom), and the support structures that new leaders require are implemented.

Chapter 3, "Mentoring Reflection: Teaching Pre-Service Teachers to Ask Why", by Latricia Trites, examines the use and perceived effectiveness of weekly reflective journals in a pre-service teacher training program at a regional university in the United States and references her research on a co-teaching program in Taiwan. Reflective journaling was developed as part of a "multi-dimensional mentoring model" (Trites & Tseng, 2009). The chapter explores the strengths and weaknesses of reflective journaling and addresses concerns that teachers, their mentors, and supervisors face as they complete and respond to reflective assignments as a component of a teacher training assessment. It looks at perceptions of these activities as required tasks, as opposed to journals that are used to develop strong relationships among teachers and their mentors as the teachers develop leadership skills. Finally, it examines how the implementation of a more dialogic approach to reflective practices can provide a framework on which to build effective teaching and teacher leadership development practices.

Chapter 4, "Co-leadership through Dialogue and Reflective Writing in the Teaching Practicum", by Carla Reichmann, discusses professional voice construction in reflective internship reports produced by undergraduate English as a Foreign Language (EFL) student teachers during their practicum in Northeast Brazil, at the Adalgisa Cunha Institute for the Blind in Paraíba. Bearing in mind that the participants are the author's students at a public university, co-supervised by the cooperating teacher at the Institute for the Blind, the author discusses the student teachers' writing in regards to classroom observation and teaching, in light of Freirean and Bakhtinian perspectives. The chapter highlights the importance of putting in place a community of practice (with all of the teachers involved) to enhance dialogue, reflective writing, and leadership development. The analysis focuses on identity and co-leadership issues that are unveiled in the student teachers' texts, suggesting the need for teacher leadership development.

Chapter 5, "Visions and Realities: Doctoral Perspectives on Practice and Leadership", by Jill Burton, examines the extent to which doctoral students in English language teaching (ELT) in one Australian university incorporated reflection in their research processes and doctoral writing. As a supervisor and doctoral student herself, Burton observes differences in how they and she approached research design and writing. The students were ELT educators, mainly in leadership roles in Southeast Asia. Using her own doctoral experience, which employed a reflective-writing methodology, she critiques the relationship between reflective writing practices and leadership to argue that teachers need to own how teaching is communicated and that true professional renewal depends on teachers as individuals leading renewal in their own settings.

Chapter 6, "Patterns of Participation in Reflective Writing and Their Implications for Teacher Leadership Development", by Joy Kreeft Peyton and Phil Quirke, considers opportunities for reflective writing in contexts of change, where teachers receive guidance and support from administrators and the education infrastructure as they emerge as leaders. The chapter describes patterns of participation in reflective writing and its impact on organizational change and leadership development, based on the written reflections of specific communities of teachers and teacher leaders in different countries of the world, including the countries represented in other chapters of this book. It examines participation in and reactions to reflective writing and individuals' learning from it as observed in their use of new knowledge and skills and their consideration of themselves as leaders. The patterns found in this study have specific implications for the use of reflective writing to promote leadership development in many different countries and educational contexts.

Chapter 7, "Reflective Writing to Develop Teacher Leaders: Where to Go from Here", by all of the authors, concludes the book with a consideration of future directions and implications for written reflective inquiry in the leadership education of language teachers. It brings together insights from the chapters in this book and suggests ways that readers might individually and collaboratively want to explore further in their own settings the roles, challenges, and complexities of implementing reflective writing to promote leadership development. Second, as an illustration, it describes a program of research on reflective writing that the authors plan to pursue to continue to develop themselves and with others as teacher leaders. It concludes with the reflection that we as a field might move forward together in this realm and that all professional activities involved in teaching and teacher education have the potential to engage individuals in becoming leaders. Most crucially, it argues that reflective writing activities encourage teachers lifelong learners to become responsible for their own development, to support a sense of responsibility in their students, and to develop ways to collaborate with colleagues and make connections in the arenas that make sense for them.

References

Albanese, D., Burr, L., Collins, T., Erlewine, M., Goshe, J., Louie, M., & Tseng, J. (2009). Three C's for a supportive educational environment: Co-teaching, cohort, and community. In C. Ward (Ed.), *Anthology series 50*. SEAMEO Regional Language Centre.

Atkinson, T., & Claxton, G. (Eds.). (2003). *The intuitive practitioner: On the value of not always knowing what one is doing.* Open University Press.

Bailey, K., Curtis, A., & Nunan, D. (1998). Undeniable insights: The collaborative use of three professional development practices. *TESOL Quarterly, 32*, 542–556.

Barnard, R., & Burns, A. (Eds.). (2012). *Language teacher education: Cognition and practice.* Multilingual Matters.

Bolton, G. (2018). *Reflective practice: Writing and professional development* (5th ed.). Sage.

Burns, A., & Burton, J. (Eds.). (2008). *Language teacher research in Australia and New Zealand.* Teachers of English to Speakers of Other Languages.

Burton, J. (2005). The importance of teachers writing on TESOL. *TESL-EJ, 9*(2), 1–18. http://tesl-ej.org/ej34/a2.pdf

Burton, J. (2009). Reflective writing – Getting to the heart of teaching and learning. In J. Burton, P. Quirke, C. Reichmann, & J. K. Peyton (Eds.), *Reflective writing: A way to lifelong teacher learning* (pp. 1–11). TESL-EJ online journal. http://www.tesl-ej.org/wordpress/books

Burton, J. (2013). An informal community of language teachers writing reflectively. In C. L. Reichmann (Ed.), *Teaching, writing, and self-making: Teacher journals and literacies [Diarios reflexivos de professors de linguas: Ensinar, escrever, refazer (-se)]* (pp. 285–300). Pontes Editores.

Burton, J., & Carroll, M. (2001). Journal writing as an aid to self-awareness, autonomy, and collaborative learning. In J. Burton & M. Carroll (Eds.), *Journal writing* (pp. 1–7). Teachers of English to Speakers of Other Languages (TESOL).

Burton, J., Quirke, P., Reichmann, C., & Peyton, J. K. (2009). (Eds.). *Reflective writing: A way to lifelong teacher learning.* TESL-EJ, E-Book Edition. http://tesl-ej.org/books/reflective_writing.pdf

Bush, T. (2011). *Theories of educational leadership and management.* Sage Publications.

Chacón, C. T. (2018). Reflective teaching. In J. I. Liontas (Ed.), *The TESOL encyclopedia of English language teaching.* John Wiley & Sons. doi:10.1002/9781118784235.eelt0211

Clandinin, J., & Connelly, F. M. (2000). *Narrative inquiry: Experience and story in qualitative research.* Jossey-Bass.

Fairclough, M. (1992). *Discourse and social change.* Policy Press.

Farrell, T. S. C. (2007). *Reflective language teaching: From research to practice.* Continuum Press.

Farrell, T. S. C. (2013). *Reflective writing for language teachers.* Equinox.

Farrell, T. S. C. (2018). Second language teacher education and future directions. In J. I. Liontas (Ed.), *The TESOL encyclopedia of English language teaching.* John Wiley & Sons. doi:10.1002/9781118784235.eelt0922

Fiedler, F. E., & Garcia, J. E. (1987). *New approaches to effective leadership: Cognitive resources and organizational performance.* Wiley.

Freire, P. (1970). *Pedagogy of the oppressed.* Seabury Press.

Fullan, M. G., with Stiegelbaker, S. (1993). *The new meaning of educational change* (2nd ed.). Teachers College Press.

Gadamer, H. G. (1976). *Philosophical hermeneutics* (D. E. Linge, Ed. & Trans.). University of California Press.

Gallup-Rodríguez, A., & McKay, S. (2010). *Professional development for experienced teachers working with adult English language learners.* Center for Applied Linguistics. http://www.cal.org/caelanetwork/resources/experienced.html

Grossman, P. (1990). *The making of a teacher: Teacher knowledge and teacher education.* Teachers College Press.

Guskey, T. (2000). *Evaluating professional development.* Corwin Press.

Hall, P., & Simeral, A. (2017). *Creating a culture of reflective practice: Capacity building for schoolwide success.* Association for Supervision and Curriculum Development.

Halliday, M. A. K. (1994). *An introduction to functional grammar* (2nd ed.). Arnold.

Hargreaves, A., & Fullan, M. (2012). *Professional capital: Transforming teaching in every school.* Teachers College Press.

He, Y. (2013). Developing teachers' cultural competence: Application of appreciative inquiry in ESL teacher education. *Teacher Development, 17*(1), 55–71.

Heidegger, M. (1982). *The basic problems of phenomenology* (A. Hofstadter, Trans.). Indiana University Press. (Original work published 1975)

Husserl, E. (1931). *Ideas: General introduction to pure phenomenology.* Macmillan.

Kotter, J. P. (1990). What leaders really do. *Harvard Business Review, 68*(3), 103–111.

Lortie, D. C. (2002). *Schoolteacher: A sociological study* (2nd ed.). University of Chicago Press.

Marques, J., & Dhiman, S. (Eds.). (2017). *Leadership today: Practices for personal and professional performance.* Springer. doi:10.1007/978-3-319-31036-7

Martin, J. R., & Rose, D. (2003). *Working with discourse.* Continuum.

Merleau-Ponty, M. (1964). *The phenomenology of perception.* Routledge & Kegan Paul.

Moon, J. A. (2004). *Reflection in learning and professional development: Theory and practice.* Routledge.

Moon, J. A. (2006). *Learning journals: A handbook for reflective practice and professional development.* Routledge.

Murphy, T., & Sato, K. (Eds.). (2005). *Communities of supportive professionals.* Teachers of English to Speakers of Other Languages.

Noffke, S. E., & Brennan, M. (2005). The dimensions of reflection: A conceptual and contextual analysis. *International Journal of Progressive Education, 3*(1), 1–34.

Olsen, B. (2010). *Teaching for success: Developing your teacher identity in today's classroom.* Paradigm.

Olsen, B. (2012). Identity theory, teacher education, and diversity. In J. Banks (Ed.), *Encyclopedia of diversity* (pp. 1122–1125). Sage.

Orem, R. (2001). Journal writing in adult ESL: Improving practice through reflective writing. *New Directions for Adult and Continuing Education, 90,* 69–78.

Peyton, J. K. (2000a). *Dialogue journals: Interactive writing to develop language and literacy.* Center for Applied Linguistics. http://www.cal.org/caela/esl_resources/digests/Dialogue_Journals.html

Peyton, J. K. (2000b). Dialogue journal writing in various contexts: Some issues to consider. In J.K. Peyton, P. Griffin, W. Wolfram, & R. Fasold (Eds.), *Language in action: New studies of language in society* (pp. 492–501). Hampton Press.

Peyton, J. K. (2009). Building an international community of scholars and practitioners through e-mail journaling. In J. Burton, P. Quirke, C. Reichmann, & J. K. Peyton (Eds.), *Reflective writing: A way to lifelong teacher learning* (pp. 156–165). TESL-EJ online journal. http://tesl-ej.org/books/reflective_writing.pdf

Pomson, A. D. M. (2005). One classroom at a time? Teacher isolation and community viewed through the prism of the particular. *Teachers College Record, 107*(4), 783–802.

Quirke, P. (2001). Maximizing student writing and minimizing teacher correction. In J. Burton & M. Carroll (Eds.), *Journal writing* (pp. 11–22). Teachers of English to Speakers of Other Languages.

Quirke, P. (2011). Developing the foundation for DREAM management. In C. Coombe, L. Stephenson, & S. Abu-Rmaileh (Eds.), *Leadership and management in English language teaching* (pp. 67–79). TESOL Arabia.

Quirke, P. (2018). Journals. In J. I. Liontas (Ed.), *The TESOL encyclopedia of English language teaching* (pp. 5065–5113). John Wiley & Sons. doi:10.1002/9781118784235.eelt0327

Quirke, P., & Allison, S. (2008). DREAM management: Involving and motivating teachers. In C. Coombe (Ed.), *Leadership in English language teaching and learning* (pp. 186–201). University of Michigan Press.

Reichmann, C. L. (Ed.). (2013). *Teaching, writing, and self-making: Teacher journals and literacies* [*Diarios reflexivos de profesores de línguas: Ensinar, escrever, refazer-se*]. Editora Pontes.

Ricoeur, P. (1981). *Hermeneutics and the human sciences.* Cambridge University Press.

Romero, T. (2009). Reflecting through autobiographies in teacher education. In J. Burton, P. Quirke, C. Reichmann, C., & J. K. Peyton (Eds.), *Reflective writing: A way to lifelong teacher learning* (pp. 82–95). TESL-EJ online journal. http://tesl-ej.org/books/reflective_writing.pdf

Rosen, H. (1996). Meaning-making narratives: Foundations for constructivist and social constructionist psychotherapies. In H. Rosen & K. T. Kuehlwein (Eds.), *Constructing realities: Meaning-making perspectives for psychotherapists* (pp. 3–49). Jossey-Bass.

Ryals, S. (2014, April 1). I'm one of the worst teachers in my state [Blog]. https://www.salon.com/2014/03/31/im_one_of_the_worst_teachers_in_my_state

Sabah, S., & Rashtchi, M. (2016). Critical thinking in personal narrative and reflective journal writings by in-service EFL teachers in Iran: Assessment of reflective writing. *Journal of Teaching Language Skills, 35*(3), 157–182.

Schlichte, J., Yessel, N., & Marbler, J. (2005). Pathways to burnout: Case studies in teacher isolation and alienation. *Preventing School Failure, 50*(1), 35–41.

Schön, D. (1987). *Educating the reflective practitioner.* Jossey-Bass.

Singer-Gabella, M. (2012). Toward scholarship in practice. *Teachers College Record, 14*(8), 1–30. https://eric.ed.gov/?id=EJ1001973

Smyth, J. (1989). Developing and sustaining critical reflection in teacher education. *Journal of Teacher Education, 40*(2), 2–9.

Smyth, J. (1992). Teachers' work and the politics of reflection. *American Educational Research Journal, 20*(2), 267–300.

Spencer, S. A. (2009). The language teacher as language learner. In J. Burton, P. Quirke, C. Reichmann, & J. K. Peyton (Eds.), *Reflective writing: A way to lifelong teacher learning* (pp. 31–48). TESL-EJ online journal. http://tesl-ej.org/books/reflective_writing.pdf

Trites, L., Sroda, M. S., & Tseng, J. M. (2009). *Multi-dimensional co-teaching/mentoring model for on-the-job teacher training.* Unpublished manuscript.

Trites, L., & Tseng, J. M., (2009, June). *Multi-dimensional co-teaching/mentoring model for on-the-job teacher training.* Paper presented at the Independent Learning Association Conference, Hong Kong.

Van Manen, M. (2007). Phenomenology of practice. *Phenomenology & Practice, 1*(1), 11–13. https://www.researchgate.net/publication/228480543_Phenomenology_of_Practice

Vygotsky, L. S. (1978). *Mind in society.* MIT Press.

Wallace, M. J. (1991). *Training foreign language teachers: A reflective approach.* Cambridge University Press.

Watanabe, A. (2016). *Reflective practice as professional development: Experiences of teachers of English in Japan.* Multilingual Matters.

Wenger, E. (1998). *Communities of practice: Learning, meaning, and identity.* Cambridge University Press.

Wenger, E., McDermott, R., & Snyder, W. (2002). *Cultivating communities of practice.* Harvard Business School Press.

Wink, J., & Putney, L. (2002). *A vision of Vygotsky.* Allyn & Bacon.

Wu, H. F., Martin, R., & Herbert, P. (2008, March). Professionalism of native and non-native English language teachers in Taiwan and its implications on collaborative teaching. In *Proceedings of the 10th international conference on TEFL and applied linguistics* (pp. 750–754). Ming Chian University.

Zeichner, K. M., & Liston, D. E. (1996). *Reflective teaching: An introduction.* Lawrence Erlbaum.

CHAPTER 2

An Approach to Using Reflective Writing to Develop Teacher Leaders: DREAM Management

Phil Quirke

This chapter focuses on the application of the DREAM Management approach to leadership development originally developed by Quirke (2008), drawing on participant reflections and contributions to synchronous and asynchronous discussions from a variety of DREAM Management courses run over the past five years. It is a structured framework with potential for use in settings other than higher education, for which it was originally developed.

The chapter describes
- the theoretical framework for and components of the DREAM Management approach and how its principles can be applied to contexts in which teachers are emerging as leaders (e.g., as mentors, professional developers, coaches, administrative support leaders, teacher educators, managers, and researchers);
- the content, forms, and importance of reflective writing in DREAM Management leadership courses;
- how current theories of teacher leadership are covered in the DREAM Management approach;
- ways to promote depth of reflection in the writing.

The framework for educational management and leadership training used in this book is based on the acronym DREAM (Quirke, 2011; Quirke & Allison, 2008, 2010; Quirke & Humeidan 2014). The DREAM educational management philosophy places teachers at the core of the educational institution and students at the heart of every decision we make and everything we do. The focus at the institutional level is to create and maintain an environment conducive to collaborative learning with and for students (Wells & Chang Wells, 1992) and faculty. This statement of focus can be deconstructed as follows:
- *environment* comprises a complex web of interrelationships, which can be positively shaped (Farrell, 2008) socially, intellectually, and emotionally (Atkinson & Claxton, 2003; Wright, 2005) through decisive actions that support teaching and learning.

- *conducive to* includes all factors essential to learning with a focus on both students inside and outside the classroom and faculty professional development and research.
- *collaborative* addresses the social constructivist nature of learning (Grossman, 1990; McNiff, 1992; Rosen, 1996; Vygotsky, 1978; Wink & Putney, 2002) and focuses attention on team building, group formation, and creation of effective, sustainable communities (Farrell, 2008).
- *with students and faculty* indicates the importance of involving students in management and ensuring that they are central in everything we do, consider, and plan for (Fennimore, 2002).
- Finally, *for students and faculty* emphasizes the need to focus on individual students and teachers, groups of students and faculty, and the whole student and teacher body when shaping learning environments (Farrell, 2008).

The DREAM Management approach embodies the following ten principles, which ensure that teachers and students are central to educational management and leadership processes, with students at the heart of a structured, practical, focused, and effective system of learning.
- *D*evelop and *D*elegate
- *R*ecruit and *R*espect
- *E*nhance and *E*njoy
- *A*ppraise and *A*ttend
- *M*otivate and *M*entor

For this book, we investigate the role of reflective writing in a new arena, the DREAM approach to educational management and leadership development.

The DREAM approach draws on the work of authors such as Fullan (1993), Hargreaves et al. (2001), and Southworth (2004), who have all emphasized the importance of bottom-up professional renewal, school-based development, learning-centered leadership, and individual responsibility in teaching and educational leadership. The literature on journal writing also provides a rich basis for this work (e.g., Burton & Carroll, 2001; Burton et al., 2009; Farrell, 2012). Here we describe the ten principles of DREAM management and show how reflective writing, individually and within and across teams, can enhance effective teacher leadership development.

1   Theoretical Structure of the Course

Social constructivists from neurological and biological studies (Maturana, 2012), teacher studies (Darling-Hammond, 2016), and knowledge management (Serenko & Dumay, 2015) demonstrate that our construction of knowledge is dependent on the environment that surrounds us, the people within that environment, and our communication with them, so that knowledge is held by the community and constructed by those within the community. These social constructivist theories view knowledge as a collective, communicative process fully dependent on the community and their interaction, with meaning constructed from our experience.

According to Beattie (1997, p. 126) learning to teach "requires experiences and settings which support reflection, collaboration, relational learning, and the creation of communities of inquiry". It also requires understanding that "a professional knowledge of teaching has many dimensions – cognitive, social, organizational, practical, moral, aesthetic, personal, political, and interpersonal" (Beattie, 1997, p. 126). Therefore, we are part of a teacher knowledge constructing community. The DREAM Management course is structured around these social constructivist theories and is based heavily upon the work of Tsui (2003), who brought together the proliferation of teacher knowledge terminology into a coherent whole, and Quirke (2009), who further developed her work into an extended model of teacher knowledge development, shown in Figure 2.1.

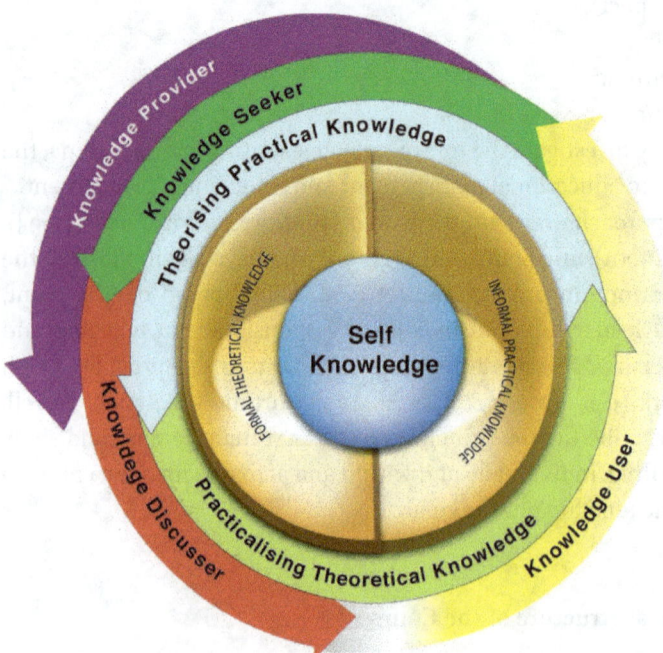

FIGURE 2.1   Model of teacher knowledge development (from Quirke, 2009)

Working from the centre of this model outwards, 'Self Knowledge' has been highlighted in both teacher education programs that focus on the individual's knowledge from the outset and in the literature on teacher knowledge (Bailey et al., 2001; Elbaz, 2016; Johnson & Golombek, 2002; Wallace, 1991).

'Informal Practical Knowledge' is based on classroom experiences in local contexts, and 'Formal Theoretical Knowledge' is the theoretical, empirical knowledge of content and pedagogy that is widely accepted by professional bodies.

'Theorizing Practical Knowledge' is the search for the formal theoretical knowledge that they can be aligned to experience, and 'Practicalizing Theoretical Knowledge' is the search for and application of new classroom practices that are grounded in theories, which are often newly articulated and part of classroom-based research. It is this continual cycle of theorizing practical knowledge and practicalizing theoretical knowledge that creates the model of teacher knowledge development. This acknowledges the complexity of teacher knowledge, the circularity of knowledge growth through practice and theoretical input, and the centrality of the local situation.

The 'Knowledge Seeker' phase mirrors the theorizing of practical knowledge. We have an understanding of ourselves, our situation, and our teaching context, and we begin to explore how we can deepen that understanding through reading, professional workshops, and further study. We are, in effect, beginning to theorize our existing practice; and by seeking new knowledge, we gain a better understanding of what we are doing through research and reflection. The changes to our existing knowledge schema triggered by reflection on newly acquired knowledge are seldom complete until we have involved others. As we shift our schema, we need confirmation from those professional colleagues around us whom we respect, as represented by the 'Knowledge Discusser' phase. We discuss how this new knowledge maps onto our existing cognitive knowledge map and decide whether or not the change we are considering for our schema is, in fact, compatible with our professional context. Key to the transformation of our knowledge structure is the 'Knowledge User' phase, which mirrors the practicalizing of theoretical knowledge as we confirm our beliefs in practice. Eventually, as our knowledge grows, we begin to realize that we have something to offer the professional community and begin to act as knowledge providers. The cycle does not end here, since a natural continuation of knowledge provision is a realization of how much more we have to learn, so we begin to seek new knowledge in a process of lifelong learning. The cycle continues and grows. The final 'Knowledge Provider' phase in this cyclical model of teacher knowledge is the key reporting element, which often strengthens our knowledge structure and beliefs, potentially moving them to the central core of our professional selves. It is this cyclical model of teacher knowledge development that informs the structure of each unit within the DREAM Management courses.

There are 11 DREAM Management courses: an introductory overview of the approach and one course for each of the 10 principles. Each course is divided into 12 units and requires approximately 40 hours of synchronous and asynchronous work. Each unit is divided into 4 stages based upon the 4 phases in the cyclical model of teacher knowledge development:

1. Knowledge Seeker: Preparatory reading or viewing of theoretical content. This is the stage in which the participants are introduced to the different educational management and leadership theories that underpin the principle.
2. Knowledge Discusser: A one-hour session on how the different management and leadership theories introduced in the previous stage might be applied to the participants' work contexts and situations. This synchronous discussion concludes with the setting of a task for the following stage and continues throughout the unit asynchronously via a forum such as the LMS Discussion Board or WhatsApp group.
3. Knowledge User: A task relevant to all the participants' specific local professional work contexts, as agreed on in the previous stage, requiring the application of the management and leadership theories of the principle.
4. Knowledge Provider: A referenced reflection on the outcomes of the task set in the previous stage, the application of the management and leadership theories, and the learning that took place during the unit.

The next section reviews the forms of reflective writing that the participants are exposed to during the courses.

2 Forms of Reflective Writing in Teacher Leader Development

Chapter 1 outlines seven personal forms of reflective writing that can be combined with four different interactive forms to give a variety of choice in the way the knowledge provider tasks can be presented. Over the years, almost every combination of these has been used in the DREAM Management leadership development courses, with different participants and groups allowed to continue working in the form with which they are most comfortable and confident.

The reflective writing tasks set at the beginning of the courses draw on a number of the forms described in Chapter 1, and the most popular and effective form chosen has been a guided reflective journal. This involves individual reflection on an experience, which starts with a narrative description of the task undertaken and an analysis of the critical incidents that resulted. The guidance then requires a reflection on the relationships between the task and the incidents described and the management and leadership theories discussed in the unit. Finally, the participants reflect on their individual, emerging educational leadership philosophy. The tutor responds to each reflection during the course, thereby constructing an ongoing leadership development conversation. As each course progresses, participants can choose their preferred forms of reflective writing and may also decide to construct the conversation with another participant or even initiate an interactive reflective writing group.

The remainder of this chapter describes how this structured reflective process has been applied in a variety of DREAM Management courses and how participants have developed their awareness of educational management and leadership theories as they have put the principles into practice.

2.1   *Educational Management and Leadership*

The clearest distinctions between management and leadership in an educational setting have been made by Cuban (1988) and Bush (1998). Cuban (1988) ties leadership with change and management with maintenance, whereas Bush (1998) links leadership to values and purpose and management to implementation. However, more recently Bush (2011) and Gunter (2004) have clarified that the field of educational leadership was initially defined as 'educational administration', later as 'educational management', and only more recently as 'educational leadership'. So, the author argues that the DREAM Management principles are consistent with the literature on educational leadership and offer effective approaches to implementing leadership values, purpose, and change through the implementation of sound management strategies and focused, values-driven action. This is demonstrated throughout the course with the unit on the Attend principle, which draws heavily on the literature from values-based leadership, and the introduction unit, which begins the course with a review of the literature on learning-centred leadership (Southworth, 2004) and appreciative inquiry (Cooperrider & Whitney, 2005). It is also clearly evidenced in the unit on the Develop principle, which focuses on the development of strategic plans at the institutional, divisional, departmental, and team levels.

2.1.1   Develop

The DEVELOP principle emphasizes the importance of collaborative planning and collective, communicative approaches to organizational development and change management to support teachers' work and student learning

(Christison & Murray, 2009; Cooperrider & Whitney, 2005). It also highlights the dispositions, behaviors, and interactions that create a positive ethos for the work that individuals and groups are engaged in (Scrivener, 2012, p. 232). DEVELOP aims to heighten the individuals' and group's awareness of their progress towards the goals they have set and the specific organizational structures and leadership strategies that can help them achieve those goals (Kaplan, 2009; Kaplan & Norton, 1992, 1996). This collaborative approach to strategic planning and making explicit links between individual strengths and goals and the institution's strategic plan had not been experienced previously by many of the participants in DREAM Management courses, which generated an early depth of reflection that formed a springboard for the rest of the course.

The references to Kaplan, above, are directly related to the Balanced Scorecard and Key Performance Indicators (KPI) approach seen today in many educational institutions, including the one in which many of the DREAM participants worked in the United Arab Emirates (UAE). This Balanced Scorecard and KPI approach to strategic planning has resulted in many educational institutions taking a top-down approach to strategic planning that involves the development of a vision with strategic goals to attain that vision and specific key performance indicators for divisions, departments, and even individuals to meet. These strategic goals and key performance indicators are then driven down through the institution with the attainment of these KPIs and then used by individuals at the executive level to measure the institution's achievement of the targeted strategic goals and realization of the vision. This kind of strategic planning, adopted from the business world, has frequently been decried as the corporatization of higher education (Berg & Seeber, 2016; Collini, 2012; Côté & Allahar, 2011; Donoghue, 2008; Ginsberg, 2011; Gould, 2014) and English language teaching (Block & Cameron, 2002; Hargreaves, 2003).

The DREAM Management courses focus on developing teacher leaders within the contexts they are working, so the focus is on turning a top-down approach to strategic management into one that is teacher-focused and allows teacher leaders to give their faculty the opportunity to select their individual goals, based on their students' interests and needs and their own teaching strengths and classroom research interests. These self-selected teacher goals can then be aligned to the key performance indicators imposed on the division, department, or individual. This teacher-centered focus of the first principle sets the tone for the course and highlights the key features of the DREAM Management approach.

The Knowledge Seeker preparatory readings for the unit on DEVELOP contrast the Balanced Scorecard approach of Kaplan and Norton and how it has been applied in Transformational (Bass & Riggio, 2006) and Transactional Leadership models with democratic leadership theories (Woods, 2005).

The Knowledge Discusser session provides a best practice model from my own leadership experience in colleges in the UAE entitled 'Strategic Planning Days Involving Everyone from Drivers to the Director'. The model outlines how the agenda for the Strategic Planning Day is based on strategic goals and KPIs, but these are only introduced in the afternoon once individual cross-disciplinary teams have settled on their individual and team goals based on their students, their strengths, and their interests. The afternoon is then spent aligning these to the KPIs in new teams, with one member recording the details that are then collated by the management team and distributed to everyone for review and refinement. The discussion revolves around how this democratic leadership process fulfills the top-down needs of the institution and works powerfully in both a transactional and transformational manner.

The Knowledge User task requires participants to present the model to their faculty and work with them on refining their teaching, learning, research, administrative, and professional development goals so that they align more closely with the institution's vision, strategic goals, and key performance indicators.

The Knowledge Provider reflections tend toward a focus on previous bad experiences with top-down management approaches or the participant's inability to do the task in their institution or department. This allows the tutor to respond and highlight three of the key concepts of DREAM Management, namely that we can control what we are held directly responsible for, that this will involve professional growth, and that we can allow our faculty to have the same levels of control as we have. The aim of these responses is to ensure that each participant gains valuable, more complex insights into the positivity and empowerment of the DREAM Management approach. As one participant concluded in her reflection following a session with her faculty, "I found the collaborative approach to identifying faculty goals and collectively having input into our mission/vision … very empowering".

3   Participation Patterns in Reflective Writing for Teacher Leader Development

Chapter 1 introduces the adaptation by the authors in this book of Guskey's (2000) framework and how it can be applied to reflective writing research to provide a rich understanding of teacher growth and teacher leader development. The next two principles of the DREAM Management course demonstrate how the six features of writing have been addressed in participant reflections. Evidence of these six features (participation patterns, participant reactions, participant learning, participant use of new knowledge and skills, organization change and support, and student learning) in the reflective writing of the participants indicates a depth of understanding, development, and professional growth.

4 Recruit

The RECRUIT principle focuses on building and enhancing collaborative teams and targeting those that can add value to the group by providing more flexibility and strength to face the fast-paced change of the world we live in today.

The Knowledge Seeker preparatory readings, therefore, focus on theories of change and leading in a culture of change (Christison & Murray, 2009; Fullan, 2006, 2016; Hargreaves et al., 2001) and adaptive leadership (Heifetz et al., 2009) and the essential role that recruitment and the building of departmental and school teams plays in creating an effective culture of learning.

The Knowledge Discusser session is framed around six key stages of the recruitment process – Expressions of Interest, Job Descriptions, Screening, Interviewing, Onboarding, and Retention – asking participants to draw on their experiences as screeners reviewing applications, interviewers, and mentors for new teachers, applicants, and new hires. Every participant had experience with at least three of these roles, and the division of the discussion around the six stages produced lively debate due to the variety of experiences, both positive and negative. This noteworthy increase in participation in the synchronous discussion continued in the asynchronous discussion forums (Participation Patterns) and was largely due to the familiarity that participants felt with the stages of the process

The Knowledge User tasks ranged from screening applications, preparing for interviews, reviewing interview questions, and exploring techniques for identifying applicants compatible with the departmental team. Further tasks included a review of mentoring approaches for orienting and training new faculty (Henderson & Noble, 2015) and suggesting other ways of increasing faculty retention. Every course has seen participants choose a different combination of two or three tasks, and ongoing asynchronous discussions while doing the tasks have seen some of the highest number of contributions, demonstrating significant depth of detail and reflection (Participant Reactions).

The Knowledge Provider reflections in the RECRUIT units demonstrated significant learning and depth of reflection, with many participants cross referencing posts on the discussion forums to describe knowledge and skills acquired during the unit (Participant Learning). The reflections in this unit were often the first to articulate how the participant felt they could initiate change in current processes, demonstrating a sense of both confidence and empowerment. Many participants stated that this was due to the fact that the unit explicitly addressed an essential area of organizational process that they were directly involved in and that they felt they could contribute to due to their experience and knowledge. The reflections also began to demonstrate independent research, with participants citing literature that had not been part of the readings but had been discovered as part of their own research while doing the task or investigating new literature to support their reflections (Participant Use of New Knowledge and Skills). For example, one participant suggested that their institution review job descriptions to include more emphasis on practitioner research rather than focus exclusively on instruction:

> More attention to the importance of practitioner's research is essential if "the UAE seeks to have its higher education institutions compete for quality and prestige in the international arena" (Austin et al., 2014, p. 545). ... It is therefore necessary to give faculty more academic flexibility (Gappa et al., 2007).

Interestingly, the institution now has research explicitly included in their job descriptions, and support for research is actively promoted. This participant felt a great sense of empowerment as one of the early voices for this change and at having been heard (Organization Change and Support).

The next principle provides evidence of the final feature of participation patterns in reflective writing, that of Student Learning.

4.1 *Enhance*

The ENHANCE principle focuses on individual teacher responsibility and professional development. The key role of the teacher leader is to value thoughtfulness and encourage teachers to reflect on their practice while also supporting individual commitment, agency, and creativity. In taking responsibility for their own development, teachers and leaders can have an impact on individuals and circumstances beyond their immediate purview (Schön, 1987) while gaining a deeper understanding of their teaching and their students' learning. By exercising this approach to professional agency beyond their own immediate contexts, teacher leaders and individual faculty can dramatically influence an entire school and its learning environment.

The Knowledge Seeker preparatory readings focus on the teacher knowledge development cycle (Quirke, 2009) and the qualities of teacher leaders (Coombe et al., 2008; Lieberman & Friedrich, 2010; Merideth, 2007; Yukl, 2010). These include the ability to critically reflect on their content and pedagogical knowledge and their views about the value of that knowledge and how it impacts the way they lead their teams. It also involves exploring their attitudes about themselves as teacher leaders, teachers, and learners and how those attitudes are displayed in their current workplace context.

The Knowledge Discusser session continues this exploration by investigating collaboratively the metalanguage that is used to talk knowledgeably about approaches to pedagogy and content. The discussion is framed around six ways in which participants can enhance their professional learning and development:

1. Reading – *In the next six months, I plan to read ...*
2. Writing – *I will keep a journal in which I will reflect on ...*
3. Leadership – *Over the next six months, I plan to develop my leadership skills by ...*
4. Connections – *In the next six months, I will make connections with the following educational leaders:*
5. Challenges – *I have faced the following challenges in the past 6 months and anticipate working on these challenges in the following ways: ...*
6. Strengths – *I consider my greatest strengths to be ... , and I can use these strengths to address the challenges I am facing in the following ways: ...*

The Knowledge User task asks participants to develop their own professional development plans with reference to their work settings, personal goals, and the preparatory readings and focus on promoting teacher collaboration and engagement with professional development in their teams. The participants are encouraged to continue the discussion asynchronously while they work on their professional development plans and expected to review their progress at the end of the course in the final reflections. The aim is to create an ongoing forum for collaborative professional development that will allow participants to develop the confidence to share their achievements and insights with others both throughout the course and long after it has finished.

The Knowledge Provider reflections in the ENHANCE units provide some of the best examples of in-depth reflections that demonstrate student learning, with reference to theories and readings from both the course and additional participant research. Use of the professional development leadership plans and the reflections on them gave clear evidence of collaborative professional development not only among the course participants, but also within the teams they were leading. There was also clear evidence of the impact that these collaborative professional development projects were having on student learning. For example, one participant reflected on his work with his teaching team on blogs and how this will impact student learning throughout the remote desert region in which he was working:

> I also want to move through more 'user like' iterations of my work on blogs. I have spent the last year piloting and indeed promoting blogs amongst other faculty. This has been through a combination of how to use the technology but also how this technology affects pedagogy and the results have been positive. I now want to start to gather more best practice from my peers and set up a group blog in which faculty can blog about blogging, with a view to improving my own blog use and to come up with a set of practical guidelines that will make blogging a more satisfying experience for all our students.

Most impressively, the participant completed this blog and the resultant guidelines, and these are still in use throughout his college setting, with students being provided with some of the best distance and online support I have witnessed (Student Learning).

The next section reviews how the Reflective Writing Typology described in Chapter 1 has been used with teachers to develop deeper perspectives, knowledge, and skills on educational management and leadership.

5   Developing Depth in Reflective Writing for Teacher Leadership Development

The Reflective Writing Typology developed by Burton (2005, 2009) presents reflective writing as a series of steps that move teachers from simple description of what happens in teaching to deeper theorizing. Throughout the DREAM Management courses, the typology is used to encourage participant ever-deepening reflections about themselves, their students, and their situations. Feedback on participants' writing seeks to consciously move participant reflections toward more complex writing and thought. The typology is used to analyze written reflections to determine the levels of reflection employed and then frame feedback questions so that participants respond at the next level of reflection. The section below on the APPRAISE principle looks at how this has been applied.

5.1   *Appraise*

The APPRAISE principle reviews strategies such as observations that can be applied formatively and positively to value teaching practices and encourage the theorizing of practical classroom knowledge and the practicalizing of new theoretical knowledge in the classroom setting. Appraisal strategies involve teachers in valuing and assessing both their own and others' teaching in a constructive manner throughout their careers. All stakeholders, including leaders, teachers, and students, should be involved in the planning, appraisal, and reflection processes, which must be clearly articulated and acceptable to all participants and employed individually and collaboratively (Ambrose et al., 2010). This approach is transparent and promotes first confidence and then commitment, because appraisal based on grounded decision making emphasizes professional development and growth rather than summative evaluation or punitive measurement.

The Knowledge Seeker preparatory readings encourage the participants to explore the wealth of literature on appraisal processes (e.g., Firestone, 2014; Murphy et al., 2013; Quirke, 2007) and think about how these are applied or not applied in their work setting.

The Knowledge Discusser session begins by emphasizing that the key to the DREAM management approach is openness and transparency and establishes that the aim of the unit is to explore different appraisal processes and give participants the confidence to apply them in their context. The session then explores a range of observation, student evaluation, and teaching portfolio approaches and asks how these can be applied to institutional requirements such as goal completion, KPI achievement, and authority compliance.

The Knowledge User task requires participants to discuss the new approaches with their faculty, apply a new method with a willing teacher, and then describe the experience in their reflection.

Therefore, and hardly surprisingly, the Knowledge Provider reflections went into substantial detail about what happened (Type 1 in Burton's Reflective Writing Typology – recording, expressing, "getting the story down") and how it happened (Type 2 – commenting on, attempting to explain) but often offered little beyond that. Consequently, the tutor feedback specifically targeted more in-depth reflections (Type 3 – theorizing on the story and reflection) to further learning by asking why a specific incident or phenomenon happened and what that might mean.

For example, one participant wrote:

> Delivering PD to teaching professionals is quite a tricky exercise. I have delivered an extensive amount of PD in the past and have mixed experience of it. The main issue I have found is when an institution introduces a new practice or technology, PD is required for it. The institution requires the teachers to adopt a new technology or pedagogy, and the teacher has a skills or knowledge gap.

My tutor feedback question to encourage the participant to reflect on the reasons for this more deeply asked:

> Why has this been an issue? You would think that this would usually be the easiest to deliver, as the knowledge gap is clearer to all.

The participant responded, drawing not only on their experience but on the literature as well:

> Regardless of potential benefits, resistance to such PD is a widely recognised phenomenon. Rarely do teachers immediately embrace innovation. Commonly observed behaviors range from skepticism to strong overt resistance. Therefore, before delivering PD, 'hindering factors' (Alias & Zainuddin, 2005) need to be identified, considered and addressed to mitigate resistance. One of the main hindering factors or resistance is why should teachers adopt a new practice when the one they have been using seems to work perfectly well. ... Failure to acknowledge possible resistance and take steps to overcome it will result in unsuccessful PD. Waldrop and Adams (1988) suggest it is essential that the innovation be presented as a supplementary viable alternative and not a direct replacement for a current wrong practice. Once an innovation is presented as an enforced replacement, resistance will occur.

The depth of this response was then further elaborated on, with the participant detailing how he had applied this approach with two faculty in using rubrics embedded within the institute's learning management system for assignment marking, and how they had appreciated both the time he took to guide them through the process and the resultant time they saved when marking student work.

The next principle expands on this development of depth in reflective writing by requiring participants to begin building explicit links between the different DREAM Management principles and thereby demonstrate an understanding of the overall ethos of the approach and the values behind it.

5.2   *Motivate*

The MOTIVATE principle allows participants to investigate and reflect on how each of the other principles can promote the sense of identity, agency, and commitment of their teacher teams (Olsen, 2010, 2012; Priestley et al., 2016) and provides an ideal opportunity to revisit reflections from earlier units of the DREAM Management course and promote Type 4 reflective writing (Are the earlier reflections credible/reasonable? Why? Why not? What do they mean now?).

The Knowledge Seeker preparatory readings introduce a range of motivational literature with a focus on Maslow's (1970) five levels of motivation related to individual needs; Alderfer's (1972) Existence, Relatedness, and Growth (E.R.G.) theory; and Herzberg's motivators and demotivators (Herzberg et al., 2010).

The essence of the DREAM Management philosophy and approach is that motivated teachers create an environment that is more conducive to learning through higher productivity, which ought to lead to greater levels of student success, as posited by Bess and Dee (2008) and McCaffery (2010). According to Bess and Dee (2008), when motivation is at a low point, a number of strategies can be applied to address this condition. Using Maslow's hierarchy of needs is one such approach. Alderfer's E.R.G. theory (1972), which was developed from Maslow's hierarchy of needs and applied in an educational setting in South Africa by Arnolds (2005), addressed much of the criticism of earlier motivational theories when he demonstrated one valid and reliable method of applying Maslow's theories. Once existence (E) factors, such as pay, benefits, and working conditions are satisified, employee motivation is enhanced through relatedness factors (R), which involve relationships with significant others, and growth factors (G), which allow individuals to develop their capacities.

The Knowledge Discusser session presents the hierarchy of needs starting with the first two elements – the concern for safety and physiological requirements, which involve the need for a secure and stable environment that the institution can actively promote (Grossman, 2004). The discussion focuses on how teacher leaders can actively be involved in this promotion through the principles of RECRUIT, ensuring the onboarding process is a positive and supportive one; and ATTEND, constantly demonstrating a concern for all of their team's basic welfare and being responsive to any concerns that are voiced.

Maslow's third need is the sense of belonging that refers to an individual's need for love, affection, and interaction with other people (Glasser, 1986). By focusing on the MENTOR and ENJOY principles, teacher leaders can ensure that everyone has a strong sense of belonging in an environment that inspires. The fourth level in Maslow's hierarchy refers to the need to develop self-esteem through personal achievement (Mruk, 2006), as well as social esteem through the recognition and respect that we earn from others (McBride, 2013). Therefore, teacher leaders can support their teams by focusing on the DEVELOP, ENHANCE, and RESPECT principles and setting attainable goals, providing professional development opportunities, and respecting the work and contributions that each individual makes to the success of students, the department, and the institution.

The DREAM Management approach is premised on Maslow's highest level (5), self-actualization or the need for self-fulfillment (Trotzer, 2006), the sense that teachers are always striving to reach their full potential. Self-actualization is something that teachers as committed professionals need to work on continuously throughout their lives. Therefore, teacher leaders must continually address this need through the application of the DELEGATE and APPRAISE principles to constantly create opportunities for teachers to contribute to a collaborative environment that encourages creativity and innovation.

The discussion concludes by encouraging participants as teacher leaders to motivate themselves, each other, and their teams in all of the areas discussed above and summarized here:
- The motivation of inclusion – DEVELOP
- The motivation of belonging – RECRUIT
- The motivation of personal advancement – ENHANCE
- The motivation of purpose – APPRAISE
- The motivation of responsibility – DELEGATE
- The motivation of respect – RESPECT
- The motivation of happiness – ENJOY
- The motivation of recognition – ATTEND
- The motivation of collaboration – MENTOR

The Knowledge User task requires participants to find out what motivates their team and reflect on the responses both in the ongoing asynchronous discussion and in their final reflective papers.

For the Knowledge Provider reflections, participants are asked to specifically review their earlier reflective submissions from the previous four principles and link these to the motivations given by their teams in the Knowledge User task for this unit's MOTIVATE principle. This review of earlier reflections from a new perspective generates Type 4 reflective writing, as participants build upon those previous submissions and consider the motivational factors of all the other principles. For example, one participant drew on push, pull, and power factors in their reflection at the end of the academic year:

> These past few days, everyone has been so busy with invigilation and grading that most appear to be motivated by the simple lure of crossing the finish line. Ironically, this frenetic time has also been a particularly fruitful period for identifying some of the deeper push and pull factors that galvanize, inspire and drive us on to face the next challenge lurking in the shadows. As you are well aware, many of our colleagues will be leaving after this semester. Some are leaving by choice while others are facing a sudden disruption in their lives and careers that they didn't see coming. The individuals in the first group are motivated by the attraction of another opportunity, the desire to go home, the lust for adventure or the call of retirement. These are responding to Maslow's higher needs

of belongingness, love, esteem, and self-actualization. Our less fortunate colleagues in the second group are largely terrified. They face the challenge of securing their basic needs, and many are at a loss regarding how they are going to do it.

The tutor drew on the ATTEND principle in responding:

And so, we have to be there in every way possible to support them – preparing references. Forwarding job opportunities and whatever else we can do to ease their path.

Interestingly, this depth of reflection has not been continued in the following DELEGATE unit, where a lack of familiarity with delegation for participants created a notable diffidence and reserved uptake of the DREAM Management approach to the principle.

5.3   Delegate

The DELEGATE principle addresses how individual and team roles and responsibilities can be distributed to enhance the quality and effectiveness of educational management and leadership (Harris, 2010).

The Knowledge Seeker preparatory readings focus on distributed and situational leadership theories (Hersey & Blanchard, 1988) and their importance for effective delegation.

The Knowledge Discusser session begins with a debate on whether delegation is an art or a science and advocates the use of a clear approach to delegation early in any change or management process so that teachers are empowered with real responsibility that focuses on their strengths. The discussion then concludes stating that many teachers, who have been solely responsible for their classrooms since they started teaching, often find it difficult to delegate responsibility effectively when they move into management and leadership roles.

The Knowledge User task requires participants to review all the assignments they have on their desk for the week and decide on one which they could most effectively delegate to their team. They should then delegate the job based on the discussion focusing on what to delegate, whom to delegate to, when to delegate, and how to delegate, with clear parameters; and ensure that there is no abdication of responsibility.

The initial Knowledge Provider reflections often describe the difficulties that participants faced in completing this task, including frustrations about how they could have finished the task far more quickly themselves. The tutor's response to these initial reflections and frustrations always aims to link the theories covered to the participants' local contexts and encourage perseverance until the participant can experience the benefits of good delegation practice. These responses attempt to move the initial reflection from a simple description of what happened and how it happened to an exploration of why it happened and what else could have been done to make the delegation more effective. The goal is to demonstrate that greater depth of reflection generates deeper learning. This is well evidenced in one participant's reflective essay at the end of the DELEGATE unit:

> A lot of things are easier if you just do it yourself. However, this is not a good way to be because (a) you will not develop your staff and (b) you will be burned out and stressed because it's impossible for anyone to do everything. No one should work more than the 40 hrs a week required. I don't think good leaders have any problems delegating. To give a couple of examples: ...

The participant then detailed two examples they had experienced from their Chair during the semester and the learning they had derived from these examples, concluding emphatically:

> I admired seeing this kind of delegation in action. It was ideal.

This allowed the tutor to encourage the course team leader participants to apply the Chair's approach in their own contexts over the rest of the course. This is an example of how the Knowledge Provider reflections have proven to be a powerful professional development and learning tool as participants continued to apply the ten principles in their local working contexts throughout the course and beyond.

5.4 *Respect*

The RESPECT principle is concerned with developing a culture that values the knowledge and contributions of everyone on the team and promotes and appreciates effective individual and collaborative work (Hawkins & Irujo, 2004; Heaton & Lampert, 1993). In successful communities of practice (Wenger, McDermott, & Snyder, 2002), effective collaboration stems from building a respectful environment in which any issues that arise can be discussed openly in and among teams before feelings of frustration or disrespect manifest themselves.

The Knowledge Seeker preparatory readings are drawn from theories of Values-Based Leadership (Copeland, 2014; Peregrym & Wollf, 2013), Authentic Leadership (George, 2003), and Ethical Leadership (Brown & Trevino, 2006).

The Knowledge Discusser session focuses on four key questions: What is respect? How do you show respect? When do you feel disrespect? and Why is respect important? The discussions are often well informed and animated, as can be expected from experienced teachers with a variety of collaborative working styles.

The Knowledge User task requires participants to consciously note how they show respect to their teacher teams, other faculty, leadership colleagues, staff, contract staff, and senior management, reflecting in action before they reflect in writing on this experience.

The Knowledge Provider reflections were some of the most powerful in articulating how participants' management and leadership practices are linked to theory, drawing on a combination of the readings, discussion, and task reflections in action. Many participants stated that this was due to the fact that the unit explicitly addressed an essential area of organizational behavior that is culturally influenced and seldom discussed openly. This was best exemplified by the following extract from one 2017 course participant:

> Respect for me is about the golden rule: treat others how you would like to be treated. For me that includes both students and colleagues. Bluestein (2012) writes a list of several values for dealing with difficult colleagues and I am going to go through the list and apply these to situations I have experienced at work.

The participant gave examples from the first five values of 'Consider is it really any of your business', 'Don't take it personally', 'Think ahead', 'Think of others' and 'Learn to ask for what you want' before concluding with the sixth:

> Believe in Your Own Power – Respect others, do your job well, always try your best, always be willing to help, always be willing to listen to others, get feedback, let everyone have input, try to make everyone happy, and decide by democratic decision making, all of which are also taken from Sandberg (2013) and describe best what I have tried to apply in my leadership of TESOL Arabia, course team leading at college, and catalyst leading for the communications course team across the sixteen colleges. Together, as a team, the results will be better than one person.

5.5 *Enjoy*

The ENJOY principle emphasizes positivity and the importance of humor, laughter, innovative thinking, and appreciation in educational management and leadership. It has been claimed that unless teachers are valued and enjoy teaching, they leave the profession within five years of becoming qualified to teach (Manuel & Hughes, 2006). Enjoyment lowers the affective filter (Krashen, 1982), thereby increasing engagement and agency, and it is, therefore, critical to learning, personal growth, and professional development. A strong sense of humor can mitigate most challenging situations, especially when the trials, humor, and solutions are shared. Most of all, though, the key to enjoyment is to be true to oneself (Scrivener, 2012).

The Knowledge Seeker preparatory readings and viewings include a focus on Emotional Intelligence (Goleman, 2005) and positivity (Al Maktoum, 2017; Ghaye, 2011). The work of Ghaye (2011) is used in particular to guide participant reflections for this principle with his focus on positivity, looking forward, and strengths-based reflection.

The Knowledge Discusser session models one effective strategy for promoting enjoyment with the exchange of personal stories about education experiences (Morgan & Rinvolucri, 1988) and encouraging participants to share those that are unusual and amusing. Anecdotes of interesting, gripping, frustrating, or humorous moments allow participants to see each other differently, revealing new insights into each other's personalities. The telling also promotes self-reflection and trust in groups, and the session concludes by deciding how this trust, humor, and enjoyment can be transferred to the participants' teams and local contexts.

The Knowledge User task, therefore, requires participants to consciously note how they demonstrate ENJOY around their institution and department, and what differences their focus on enjoyment made to their experiences during the week.

The Knowledge Provider reflections were particularly interesting, because they demonstrated student learning and departmental cohesion and were often positively affected by the initiatives introduced and applied during the week. For example, one participant reflected:

> Working with another class on preparation for their final test on analyzing children's writing samples, because we had gone through several samples and the students did well and worked hard, I gave them the remainder of their lesson time to work on their other assessment preparation. I felt they needed this class time to do this as they are under a lot of pressure and I wanted them to remain positive. Giving them class time to work on assessments would help to do this and ease pressure. I felt being in a positive state of mind helped me to show 'empathic concern' in sensing their needs (Goleman, 2013). Would I have done this had I not have been in such a positive mindset? ... I have tried to keep a positive mindset in all situations and interactions, particularly this week. ... For the most part being positive has had a seemingly positive impact on others.

6   Increasing Depth of Reflection through Asking Why

Throughout this chapter, examples of asking 'Why' questions have demonstrated how these can help participants move their reflections from simple description and narrative to a deeper exploration of the values, meanings, and theories behind their practice. It should be stressed that the approach to asking 'Why' questions is a structured one that ensures that the participants understand that these 'Why' questions are, as detailed in Chapter 1, truly explorations of meaning and understanding and not in any way an indication that something in the original reflection was wrong. It is these 'True Why' questions that create opportunities for depth of reflection, and the final two principles and three reflections in the course ask participants to apply the same approach in their reviews of earlier reflections.

6.1   *Attend*

The ATTEND principle focuses on qualitative and humanistic factors that typically affect day-to-day departmental decisions and actions, and emphasizes teachers coming to know themselves and each other through continually listening to what others say and recognizing each other's strengths, challenges, concerns, and future plans. In short, it entails mutual respect and the continual demonstration of respect in our daily routines.

The Knowledge Seeker preparatory readings and viewings, therefore, draw on the literature of servant leadership (Greenleaf, 2002; Sipe & Frick, 2009) and work on values-based leadership (Peregrym & Wollf, 2013).

The Knowledge Discusser session presents one strategy for applying these leadership theories to our daily management routine that uses seven techniques: Management by walking around (MBWA) and talking to everyone in the team; using calendar tools for tasks as well as appointments; coping with email overload so that Inbox, Sent, and Deleted folders are emptied to zero by the end of the week; sending emails that are no longer than one paragraph; repeating the ENJOY principle task and smiling with everyone in the team at least once a day; asking questions all week to clarify misunderstandings and ensure that we are hearing the right message; and helping someone at least once every day.

The Knowledge User task then requires the participants to implement the strategy discussed to their daily work for a full week and reflect on both the experience and previous reflections in light of these seven techniques.

The Knowledge Provider reflections give participants the opportunity to explore their earlier actions and experiences in the course, and promote Type 4 reflective writing (See Chapter 1 and Burton 2005, 2009) by questioning whether or not these earlier reflections are still considered credible and reasonable when viewed from values-based and servant leadership perspectives. One participant went through the seven techniques drawing on another principle's previous reflection for each technique and concluded:

> It was very enjoyable to do this week's task and the trick is, I think, to keep it going when you are not doing it so consciously – to make it a natural habit. ... So, for me 'attend' entails recognizing and knowing the individual person in our colleagues and to acknowledge this every day.

This extract mirrored how many participants felt about the module on the ATTEND principle, with a lot of the feedback stating that the practical nature of the seven techniques allowed them to reflect in greater depth about the theories based on the recent experience of trying to apply practical tasks on the ground.

6.2   *Mentor*

The MENTOR principle describes the guidance, support, and interpersonal relationships that should be built by teachers, supervisors, and staff as they carry out a common vision and create an environment conducive to teacher development. Mentoring is both constructive and reciprocal and encourages teachers to discuss their needs and circumstances openly and in confidence with another person who is in a position to be a positive help to them (Jonson, 2008).

A mentor may be a successful teacher with advanced language proficiency or classroom experience, who can support another teacher in unique ways. The mentoring teacher may have been at the school or in the district for some time or have specific knowledge that the team or the school needs. Mentoring relationships are easiest to set up at the beginning of a new course or year when, for example, experienced teachers are grouped with new teachers, so that the new or inexperienced teachers can be guided through the intricacies of the new institute.

The Knowledge Seeker preparatory readings focus on communities of practice (Wenger et al., 2002) and mentorship in educational settings (Jonson, 2008; Quirke & Allison, 2010). In preparation for the discussion session, participants are asked to consider how a safe environment can be created that would enable their teams to teach creatively, research actively, reflect honestly, and question their practice collaboratively.

The Knowledge Discusser session asks participants what good mentors and mentees need to do to build an effective learning relationship and how an environment can be created within their department or team that allows mentorships to flourish.

The Knowledge User task recognizes that this unit usually falls at the end of the academic year or fall semester and, therefore, asks participants to discuss potential mentorships with their teams for the coming semester and specifically choose someone they would like to mentor and someone they would like to be mentored by. These mentorships should specify the focus of the mentorship. They need not be restricted by members of the team but can branch out to any professional colleague anywhere. The golden rule is that both mentor and mentee must be willing to take the role on and be motivated to work with the other.

The Knowledge Provider reflections should draw on the reflections from earlier units when specifying the personal choice of mentor and mentee and the focus of the mentorships. Participants must, therefore, review their reflective writing from a couple of months earlier, and they are encouraged to reflect collaboratively by providing constructive feedback on each other's reflections. The aim is for participants to reflect on their earlier writing in light of subsequent experiences throughout the course and re-examine their initial theorizing in light of these intervening events, questioning how their perspectives may change when viewed through a mentoring lens focused on future development. This final unit reflection often leads to Type 5 reflective writing and displays observable increases in depth of reflection and growth of professional and leadership awareness. For example, one participant concluded a long description of their previous mentorship experiences that drew on previous unit reflections by stating insightfully:

> Conversations take time, and commitment, and genuine interest and through my most important mentoring relationships, I would say that the most benefit came to me during conversations with my mentor/mentee. These chats allowed me to consider my current situation, discuss possibilities and options, and helped me to see the bigger picture, which oftentimes is difficult. I believe that a truly good mentorship often moves into friendship, so when describing a good mentor, I can't help but feel like I am describing a good friend.

7 Conclusion

The final, concluding unit of the course requires participants to reread all their reflections before the discussion, which focuses on the learning throughout the course and how each of the participants wants to continue their educational management and leadership journey. The final reflections then require participants to draw upon their previous reflective papers while looking forward positively and continuing the discussion asynchronously. This resulted in some very strong examples of Type 5 reflective writing, with participants demonstrating increasing depth of reflection as they re-examined their earlier writings in light of their subsequent experiences throughout the course. One participant wrote:

> The DREAM management course was a model of how to lead and manage an organization. I totally appreciate the value of what was put forward. What was disappointing for me, was knowing that DREAM was the way to do things, but I was not always seeing it in practice within this organization. I can definitely see elements of the different aspects of it, which I have mentioned in my past reflections, but there has always been a slight frustration as to why everyone would not follow the model. I would hope that everyone would want to work in an environment that was positive, creative, empathetic, collaborative, respectful, appreciative etc. For me, that's what the DREAM model endorses. It seems logical and ideal. A sentiment which seemed to be shared by the majority of attendees at the weekly Zoom meetings. So, what stops people seeing the value of following the model? Why are there differences amongst the campuses?

The participant continued for another two pages, answering these questions and drawing upon her earlier reflections before looking forward to how she would like to continue working on her leadership skills.

> DREAM is about having the Emotional Intelligence [EQ] to deal with your work life and those you work with. Although I have read articles about EQ and indeed discussed and addressed it in various courses and workshops I've delivered, DREAM gave me the chance to reflect on my EQ as well as think more deeply about how it affected me within my career. I hope to take part in other DREAM courses but feel a principle each week was too much to be able to give the readings and reflections justice.

This chapter has examined one approach to using reflective writing to develop teacher leaders and, by drawing on a selection of participants' reflections, has attempted to demonstrate how the promotion of ever deepening reflection that connects practical experiences with leadership theory can provide significant learning opportunities for development.

References

Alderfer, C. P. (1972). *Existence, relatedness, and growth: Human needs in organizational settings*. Free Press.

Alias, N. A., & Zainuddin, A. M. (2005, August). Innovation for better teaching and learning: Adopting the learning management system. *Malaysian Online Journal of Instructional Technology, 2*(2), 27–40.

Al Maktoum, M. b. R. (2017). *Reflections on happiness and positivity*. Explorer Publishing.

Ambrose, S. A., Bridges, M. W., DiPietro, M., Lovett, M. C., & Norman, M. K. (2010). *How learning works: 7 research-based principles for smart teaching*. Jossey-Bass.

Arnolds, C. A. (2005). An Alderfer perspective of the higher education restructuring in South Africa. *SA Journal of Industrial Psychology, 31*(2), 22–29. doi:10.4102/sajip.v31i2.191

Atkinson, T., & Claxton, G. (Eds.). (2003). *The intuitive practitioner: On the value of not always knowing what one is doing*. Open University Press.

Austin, A. E., Chapman, D. W., Farah, S., Wilson, E., & Ridge, N. (2014). Expatriate academic staff in the United Arab Emirates: The nature of their work experiences in higher education institutions. *Higher Education, 68*(4), 541–557. doi:10.1007/s10734-014-9727-z

Bailey, K., Curtis, A., & Nunan, D. (2001). *Pursuing professional development: The self as source*. Heinle & Heinle.

Bass, B. M., & Riggio, R. E. (2006). *Transformational leadership*. Lawrence Erlbaum.

Beattie, M. (1997). Fostering reflective practice in teacher education: Inquiry as a framework for the construction of professional knowledge in teaching. *Asia-Pacific Journal of Teacher Education, 25*(2), 111–128.

Berg, M., & Seeber, B. K. (2016). *The slow professor: Challenging the culture of speed in the academy*. University of Toronto Press.

Bess, J. L., & Dee, J. R. (2008). *Understanding college and university organization: Theories for effective policy and practice*. Stylus.

Block, D., & Cameron, D. (2002). *Globalization and language teaching*. Routledge.

Bluestein, J. (2012). *Dealing with difficult colleagues*. http://www.educationworld.com/a_curr/bluestein-dealing-with-difficult-colleagues-part1.shtml

Brown, M. E., & Trevino, L. K. (2006). Ethical leadership: A review and future directions. *The Leadership Quarterly, 17*, 595–616.

Burton, J. (2005). The importance of teachers writing on TESOL. *TESL-EJ, 9*(2), 1–18. http://tesl-ej.org/ej34/a2.pdf

Burton, J. (2009). Reflective writing – Getting to the heart of teaching and learning. In J. Burton, P. Quirke, C. Reichmann, & J. K. Peyton (Eds.), *Reflective writing: A way to lifelong teacher learning* (pp. 1–11). TESL-EJ, E-Book Edition. http://www.tesl-ej.org/wordpress/books

Burton, J., & Carroll, M. (2001). Journal writing as an aid to self-awareness, autonomy, and collaborative learning. In J. Burton & M. Carroll (Eds.), *Journal writing* (pp. 1–7). Teachers of English to Speakers of Other Languages.

Burton, J., Quirke, P., Reichmann, C., & Peyton, J. K. (2009). (Eds.). *Reflective writing: A way to lifelong teacher learning.* TESL-EJ, E-Book Edition. http://tesl-ej.org/books/reflective_writing.pdf

Bush, T. (1998). The national professional qualification for headship: The key to effective school leadership. *School Leadership & Management, 18*(3), 321–334.

Bush, T. (2011). *Theories of educational leadership and management.* Sage Publications.

Christison, M. A., & Murray, D. E. (Eds.). (2009). *Leadership in English language education: Theoretical foundations and practical skills for changing times.* Routledge.

Collini, S. (2012). *What are universities for?* Penguin.

Coombe, C., McCloskey, M. L., Stephenson, L., & Anderson, N. J. (Eds.). (2008). *Leadership in English language teaching and learning.* University of Michigan Press.

Cooperrider, D. L., & Whitney, D. (2005). *Appreciative inquiry: A positive revolution in change.* Berrett-Koehler.

Copeland, M. K. (2014). The emerging significance of values based leadership: A literature review. *International Journal of Leadership Studies, 8*(2), 105–135.

Côté, J. E., & Allahar, A. (2011). *Lowering higher education: The rise of corporate universities and the fall of liberal education.* University of Toronto Press.

Cuban, L. (1988). *The managerial imperative and the practice of leadership in schools.* State University of New York Press.

Darling-Hammond, L. (2016). Research on teaching and teacher ducation and its influences on policy and practice. *Educational Researcher, 45*(2), 83–91.

Donoghue, F. (2008). *The last professors: The corporate university and the fate of the humanities.* Fordham University Press.

Elbaz, F. (1983). *Teacher thinking: A study of practical knowledge.* Croom Helm.

Farrell, T. S. C. (2008). *Classroom management.* TESOL International Association.

Farrell, T. S. C. (2012). *Reflective writing for language teachers.* Equinox.

Fennimore, B. S. (2002). *Student-centred classroom management.* Delmar Publishers.

Firestone, W. A. (2014). Teacher evaluation policy and conflicting theories of motivation. *Educational Researcher, 43*(2), 100–107.

Fullan, M. (2006). *Change theory: A force for school improvement.* Seminar Series Paper No. 157. Centre for Strategic Education, Joliment, Victoria, Australia.

Fullan, M. (2016). *The NEW meaning of educational change* (5th ed.). Teachers College Press.

Fullan, M. G., with Stiegelbaker, S. (1993). *The new meaning of educational change* (2nd ed.). Teachers College Press.

Gappa, J. M., Austin, A. E., & Trice, A. G. (2007). *Rethinking faculty work: Higher education's strategic imperative.* Jossey-Bass.

George, B. (2003). *Authentic leadership: Rediscovering the secrets to creating lasting value.* Jossey-Bass.

Ghaye, T. (2011). *Teaching and learning through reflective practice: A practical guide for positive action.* Routledge.

Ginsberg, B. (2011). *The fall of the faculty: The rise of the all-administrative university and why it matters.* Oxford University Press.

Glasser, W. (1986). *Control theory in the classroom.* Harper & Row.

Goleman, D. (2005). *Emotional intelligence: Why it can matter more than IQ.* Bantam Books.

Goleman, D. (2013). *What makes a leader: Why emotional intelligence works.* More Than Sound.

Gould, E. (2014). *The university in a corporate culture.* Yale University Press.

Greenleaf, R. K. (2002). *Servant leadership: A journey into the nature of legitimate power and greatness* (25th anniversary ed.). Paulist Press.

Grossman, P. (1990). *The making of a teacher: Teacher knowledge and teacher education.* Teachers College Press.

Grossman, H. (2004). *Classroom behavior management for diverse and inclusive schools.* Rowman & Littlefield.

Gunter, H. (2004). Labels and labelling in the field of educational leadership. *Discourse – Studies in the Cultural Politics of Education, 25*(1), 21–41.

Guskey, T. (2000). *Evaluating professional development.* Corwin Press.

Hargreaves, A. (2003). *Teaching in the knowledge society: Education in the age of insecurity.* Teachers College Press.

Hargreaves, A., Earl, L., Moore, S., & Manning, S. (Eds.). (2001). *Learning to change: Teaching beyond subjects and standards.* Jossey-Bass.

Harris, A. (2010). Distributed leadership: Evidence and implications. In T. Bush, L. Bell, & D. Middlewood (Eds.), *The principles of educational leadership & management* (2nd ed.). Sage.

Hawkins, M., & Irujo, S. (Eds.). (2004). *Collaborative conversations among language teacher educators.* Teachers of English to Speakers of Other Languages.

Heaton, R. M., & Lampert, M. (1993). Learning to hear voices: Inventing a new pedagogy of teacher education. In D. K. Cohen, M. W. McLaughlin, & J. Talbert (Eds.), *Teaching for understanding: Challenges for policy and practice* (pp. 43–83). Jossey-Bass.

Heifetz, R., Grashow, A., & Linsky, M. (2009). *The practice of adaptive leadership: Tools and tactics for changing your organization.* Harvard Business Press.

Henderson, R., & Noble, K. (2015). *Professional learning, induction and critical reflection: Building workforce capacity in education.* Palgrave Macmillan.

Hersey, P., & Blanchard, K. H. (1988). *Management of organizational behavior: Utilizing human resources.* Prentice-Hall.

Herzberg, F., Mausner, B., & Snyderman, B. B. (2010). *The motivation to work.* Transaction Publishers.

Johnson, K., & Golombek, P. (2002). *Teachers' narrative inquiry as professional development.* Cambridge University Press.

Jonson, K. F. (2008). *Being an effective mentor: How to help beginning teachers succeed.* Corwin.

Kaplan, R. S. (2009). Conceptual foundations of the balanced scorecard. *Handbooks of Management Accounting Research, 3,* 1253–1269. doi:10.1016/S1751-3243(07)03003-9

Kaplan, R. S., & Norton, D. P. (1992). The balanced scorecard: Measures that drive performance. *Harvard Business Review, 1,* 71–79.

Kaplan, R. S., & Norton, D. P. (1996). Using the balanced scorecard as a strategic management system. *Harvard Business Review, 1,* 75–85.

Krashen, S. (1982). *Principles and practice in second language acquisition.* Pergamon Press.

Lieberman, A., & Friedrich, L. D. (2010). *How teachers become leaders: Learning from practice and research.* Teachers College Press.

Manuel, J., & Hughes, J. (2006). "It has always been my dream": Exploring pre-service teachers' motivations for choosing to teach. *Teacher Development, 10*(1), 5–24.

Maslow, A. H. (1970). *Motivation and personality.* Harper & Row.

Maturana, H. (2012). Reflections on my collaboration with Francisco Varela. *Constructivist Foundations, 7*(3), 155–164.

McBride, C. (2013). *Recognition.* Polity.

McCaffery, P. (2010). *The higher education manager's handbook: Effective leadership and management in universities and colleges* (2nd ed.). Routledge.

McNiff, J. (1992). *Creating a good social order through action research.* Hyde.

Merideth, E. M. (2007). *Leadership strategies for teachers.* Corwin Press, Sage Publications.

Morgan, J., & Rinvolucri, M. (1988). *Once upon a time: Using stories in the language classroom.* Cambridge University Press.

Mruk, C. (2006). *Self-esteem research, theory, and practice: Toward a positive psychology of self-esteem.* Springer.

Murphy, J., Hallinger, P., & Heck, R. H. (2013). Leading via teacher evaluation: The case of the missing clothes? *Educational Researcher, 42*(6), 349–354.

Olsen, B. (2010). *Teaching for success: Developing your teacher identity in today's classroom.* Paradigm.

Olsen, B. (2012). Identity theory, teacher education, and diversity. In J. Banks (Ed.), *Encyclopedia of diversity* (pp. 1122–1125). Sage.

Peregrym, D., & Wollf, R. (2013). Values-based leadership: The foundation of transformational servant leadership. *The Journal of Values-Based Leadership, 6*(2), Article 7.

Priestley, M., Biesta, G., & Robinson, S. (2016). *Teacher agency: An ecological approach.* Bloomsbury Academic.

Quirke, P. (2007). A coherent approach to faculty appraisal. In C. Coombe (Ed.), *Evaluating teaching effectiveness in EFL/ESL contexts* (pp. 89–105). University of Michigan Press.

Quirke, P. (2008). Supporting teacher development on the Web. In Garton, S. & Richards, & K. (Eds.), *Professional encounters in TESOL: Discourses of teachers in training* (pp. 135–150). Palgrave.

Quirke, P. (2009). *An exploration of teacher knowledge.* VDM Publishers.

Quirke, P. (2011). Developing the foundation for DREAM management. In C. Coombe, L. Stephenson, & S. Abu-Rmaileh (Eds.), *Leadership and management in English language teaching* (pp. 67–79). TESOL Arabia.

Quirke, P., & Allison, S. (2008). DREAM management: Involving and motivating teachers. In C. Coombe (Ed.), *Leadership in English language teaching and learning* (pp. 186–201). University of Michigan Press.

Quirke, P., & Allison, S. (2010). Building leaders through mentoring. In J. A. Carmona (Ed.), *Language teaching and learning in ESL education* (pp. 179–192). Kona Publishing.

Quirke, P., & Humeidan, M. (2014). DREAM management: Empowering students through leadership training. In C. Coombe, B. Wiens, P. Davidson, & K. Cedro (Eds.), *Perspectives on student leadership development* (pp. 3–12). TESOL Arabia.

Rosen, H. (1996). Meaning-making narratives: Foundations for constructivist and social constructionist psychotherapies. In H. Rosen & K. T. Kuehlwein (Eds.), *Constructing realities: Meaning-making perspectives for psychotherapists* (pp. 3–49). Jossey-Bass.

Sandberg, S. (2013). *Lean in: Women, work, and the will to lead.* Deckle Edge.

Schön, D. (1987). *Educating the reflective practitioner.* Jossey-Bass.

Scrivener, J. (2012). *Classroom management techniques.* Cambridge University Press.

Serenko, A., & Dumay, J. (2015). Citation classics published in knowledge management journals. Part I: Articles and their characteristics. *Journal of Knowledge Management, 19*(2), 410–431.

Sipe, J. W., & Frick, D. M. (2009). *Seven pillars of servant leadership: Practicing the wisdom of leading by serving.* Paulist Press.

Southworth, G. (2004). Learning-centered leadership. In B. Davies (Ed.), *The essentials of school leadership* (pp. 91–111). Paul Chapman.

Trotzer, J. (2006). *The counselor and the group: Integrating theory, training, and practice.* Routledge.

Tsui, A. B. M. (2003). *Understanding expertise in teaching.* Cambridge University Press.

Vygotsky, L. S. (1978). *Mind in society.* MIT Press.

Waldrop, P. B., & Adams, T. M. (1988). *Overcoming resistance to the use of instructional computing in higher education.* https://eric.ed.gov/?id=ED296656

Wells, G., & Chang Wells, G. L. (1992). *Constructing knowledge together: Classrooms as centers of inquiry and literacy.* Heinemann.

Wenger, E., McDermott, R., & Snyder, W. M. (2002). *Cultivating communities of practice: A guide to managing knowledge.* Harvard Business School Press.

Wink, J., & Putney, L. (2002). *A vision of Vygotsky.* Allyn & Bacon.

Woods, P. (2005). *Democratic leadership in education.* Sage.

Wright, T. (2005). *Classroom management in language education.* Palgrave MacMillan.

Yukl, G. A. (2010). *Leadership in organizations.* Prentice Hall.

CHAPTER 3

Mentoring Reflection: Teaching Pre-Service Teachers to Ask Why

Latricia Trites

Much has been written about the different components of reflection, indicating the many characteristics that make it effective; however, research has also shown that without direct instruction and feedback, pre-service teachers (PTS) simply report on the lesson that was taught and problems that occurred without critically evaluating their part in the lesson. Research indicates that reflection needs to be dialogic, indicating a sociocultural dynamic, and that joint reflection is only effective with strong tutoring support and guided reflection (Frick, Carl, & Beets, 2010; Mauri, Clarà, Colomina, & Onrubia, 2016), showing that while teaching PTS to reflect and providing feedback is important, the interactive component is most important and that cooperating teachers (CTS) are probably best situated to provide that interaction.

Reflection is a critical component of professional development, no matter the discipline, and teaching is no exception. It allows people to be self-evaluative and to take action on that reflection. As Frick et al. (2010) state, "reflection on professional practice is one of the qualities that characterize a good teacher" (p. 422). To become a reflective teacher, one must first determine why and how to reflect. Researchers (Dewey, 1993, as cited in Farrell, 2015; Farrell, 2013, 2015, 2019; Richards & Lockhart, 1994; Schön, 1983, as cited in Azizah, Nurkanto, & Drajati, 2018) have defined different purposes and stages of reflection, including Reflection-in-Action, Reflection-on-Action, Reflection-as-Action, and Reflection-for-Action. While Reflection-in-Action is spontaneous, it requires confidence and knowledge of pedagogical strategies. Reflection-on-Action is often defined as a post-mortem to the lesson; problem solving to mitigate issues from arising the next time the lesson is taught or, as Farrell (2019) defines it, "reflection-as-repair" (p. 3). He continues that while it might help improve teaching, it might also become routinized, "reducing it to a set of recipe-following checklists and questions for teachers" (Farrell, 2019, p. 3). Reflection-for-Action is defined as reflecting on what has taken place in previous classes and, based on students' needs, preparing for upcoming lessons. Reflection-as-Action is defined as the purposeful, focused reflection that is a "way of life" as recommended by Farrell (2019, p. 31), who argues that if teachers don't actively reflect on their teaching, they can easily slip into routines and fail to enact the change that is needed (Farrell, 2013, 2015).

Researchers have studied the benefits of reflection, describing many of the characteristics of quality reflection and providing suggestions as to the best possible means of developing and maintaining a reflective state of mind (Azizah et al., 2018; Farrell, 2013, 2015; Lee, 2007; Wlodarsky, 2018). Lee (2007) explains that effective reflection needs to focus on a "constructivist approach, where teacher learners focus on what they know instead of what they do, bringing prior knowledge and personal experience to bear on the new learning situations" (p. 321). She continues by stating that quality reflection "requires critical thought, self-direction, and problem solving, coupled with personal knowledge and self-awareness" (Chant, Haefner, & Bennett, 2004; as cited in Lee, 2007, p. 321). This dialogic approach is echoed by Farrell (2013), who explains that reflection must also be evidence-based so that it connects beliefs to practices, but above all else that it become a way of life. For this to happen, PTs must be convinced that it is purposeful and not simply a required activity to be checked off a list.

While many teachers comment that writing down their reflective thoughts is time consuming, researchers support the use of diaries, journals, response/dialogue journals, and the like among teachers (Lakshmi, 2009; Peyton, 2009; Töman, 2017). Farrell (2013), Töman (2017), and Wlodarsky (2018) insist that reflection is a catalyst for teacher change and that this self-reporting provides ample evidence of effective and ineffective teaching practices, but without a record, whether written or recorded, teachers are not likely to enact change or realize their own strengths. In addition, researchers (Brandt, 2007; Ciavaldini-Cartaut, 2015; Lee, 2007) indicate that the role of a constructivist approach allows for reflection to become a collaborative effort. Through this discussion with qualified and trusted peers, teachers develop what Farrell (2015) termed as "critical friendships" (p. 22). Brandt (2007) articulates it nicely by stating that "reflective practice encourages greater self-reliance through questioning and reflection, and is suggestive of a socially-constructed view of learning that recognizes teaching as an essentially complex, interactive, and contingent activity" (p. 45).

Since reflection is so critical, questions arise as to how prepared PTs are to reflect effectively. Wlodarsky (2018) states that without focused attention, they may not be aware of the "role reflection can play in enabling and operationalizing change" (p. 34). She states, "Reflective processes take time ... and ... must reach a level of practiced engagement so that, when the pressures of decision-making emerge, the professional defaults to better quality decisions" (p. 37). Azizah et al. (2018) state that since PTs are in a constant state of development, connecting theory to practice, they need to be explicitly taught to reflect.

1 Pre-Service Teacher Disconnect

While professionals agree that reflection is critical, often PTs feel ill-equipped to reflect effectively. In addition, since they often feel powerless to enact change (Frick et al., 2010), they may feel that the reflections they are required to complete are simply time-consuming busy work and feel disconnected to the reflective process (Middleton, Abrams, & Seaman, 2011). When PTs reported using dialogue journals, it was found that they did become more reflective in the process of journaling; however, many found that the process was too time consuming, resulting in a lack of sustained practice in journaling (Lee, 2007). When examining the use of dialogue journals, some PTs perceived the whole process as simply asking experienced teachers for advice instead of a conversation about reflective teaching practices. Often, PTs buy into the "myth that reflection is simply 'just thinking hard about what you do'", which then, in turn, leads to the assumption that PTs "know how to reflect on their behavior, thoughts and feelings and that they are able to modify their decision making appropriately" (Jones & Jones, 2013, p. 82).

Middleton et al. (2011) explored PT attitudes about reflective practices, finding that often PTs resist reflection through "disidentification and resistance" (p. 68). They define disidentification as a PT who does not "fully identify as a reflective practitioner" and resistance as a PT who develops a "negative stance toward the dominant discourse" (p. 69). Resistance occurs when PTs do not perceive the effectiveness of reflection and find the reflective practice to be a required chore needed to be completed to obtain licensure. In fact, PTs often feel that reflection is too cumbersome and something that "real teachers" don't do (Middleton et al., 2011, pp. 72–73).

While PTs are required to reflect, they are most often inadequately prepared and request that both mentors and the university be more practical in training them for reflection (Frick et al., 2010: Lee, 2007; Middleton et al., 2011) by providing them with advice through "pointers, prompts, guided questions, or suggested frameworks for journal writing" (Lee, 2007, p. 328). Since PTs don't see reflective practices as something that "real teachers" do, it is critical that "real teachers" be the ones to mentor them "into understanding how reflective practices extend beyond their teacher training program into their professional careers" (Middleton et al., 2011, p. 74).

2 Limited Perspective of Cooperating Teacher/Mentors

The role of the mentor (hereafter used as synonymous with cooperating teacher, CT) is critical in that it helps PTs to develop their "professional identity" (Frick et al., 2010; Ganser, 2002). However, most CTs are selected because they are good teachers, trained teacher leaders, and benevolent souls for which no explicit training has been provided (Hudson, Nguyen, & Hudson, 2009; Sempowicz & Hudson, 2012). CTs are often only required to undergo minimal training and are provided with general guidelines and expectations, yet mentorship in reflection is typically not included. Frequently, CTs are hired because of what "comes natural", and while they feel prepared in general, the lack of formal training reflects low expectations for all involved (Ganser, 2002). The expectations that most school districts have, and that CTs perceive as their sole task, are to assist PTs by reviewing their lesson plans, observing their teaching, providing feedback and advice on those lessons, exposing them to the profession, and facilitating their ability to evaluate their own teaching practices (College of Education and Human Services Teacher Education Services, 2019). However, teaching the PT to be reflective is seldom felt to be the job of the CT.

Another issue with this lack of training is that often post-lesson sessions, in which the CT talks with the PT about the lesson, become what Ciavaldini-Cartaut (2015) describes (in the mentor-mentee sessions observed in her study) as "sterile interactions", simply a series of questions that PTs are required to answer to assist in developing teaching practices. Her research found that little to no reflection took place in many sessions, while effective post-lesson mentoring conferences included "concrete observable traces" that PTs could actually analyze. She concludes that to encourage a collaborative environment, CTs need to call "attention to the PT's motives for acting in teaching situations" (p. 497). She articulates that CTs need to ask questions and specifically direct the PT to examine their practices and to help them "deconstruct" (p. 506) the issues and recommends providing PTs with "detailed guidance" (p. 508). Ciavaldini-Cartaut (2015) indicates that, unfortunately, CTs are not able or willing to take on this task without training in ways to encourage more reflections among the PTs with whom they work.

Concerns about the CT/PT relationship reveal that there is a great disparity in the quality of CTs. Haney (1997, as cited in Hudson, Nguyen, & Hudson, 2009) defines mentoring as "a way to develop teaching practices that involve a close relationship between a less experienced person and one who is more experienced, who provides guidance, advice, support, and feedback" (p. 87). However, in research conducted by Hudson, Nguyen, and Hudson (2009), they found that PTs reported that most of the CTs in their small study did not model teaching practices appropriate to their field, did not model effective lesson planning or classroom management, and did not provide written feedback or even review the lesson plans of the PTs. In addition, many PTs have reported lacking confidence in the abilities and dedication of their CTs. On the whole, Hudson, Usak, and Savron-Gencer (2009) found that PTs felt that the CTs they worked with failed to plan for and lacked understanding of the mentoring process and that the CTs "may concentrate more on training pre-service teachers [PTs] to deliver curriculum, rather than developing them as teachers" (p. 65). They also reported that only 17% of the CTs worked with them on reflecting on their teaching practices and that CTs needed to be trained to ask probing questions that would "elicit reflective pedagogical improvements" (Hudson, Usak, & Savron-Gencer, 2009, p. 67). CTs also need to be trained to listen attentively to determine whether PTs are critically reflecting on their teaching. Since most CTs report that they do model effective lesson planning and reflection, it is important to train them to be more overt in their communication with PTs, so that these practices are more apparent to them.

3 Explicit Instruction on Reflection

As noted earlier, PTs often feel that the tasks they are assigned throughout their pedagogical training are simply classroom assignments with little bearing on their future careers, whether it be designing a lesson, unit, or assessment tool or writing a reflection on an observation or microteaching lesson. When they do observe teachers, they seldom see scripted lessons, such as the ones that students enrolled in preservice classes prior to their final student teaching experience are required to produce for the education classroom, with detailed standards and objectives articulated. While experienced teachers have ready access to these items, they are often not shared with the PT, leaving them to see the classroom tasks as cumbersome and trivial busy work.

As teacher trainers, we must pull back the curtain on the profession, allowing PTs to see that while practicing teachers have a multitude of resources at the ready, it has come with years of hard work and practice. Jones and Jones (2013) examined a university course focused on reflection in which the professor modeled reflection, provided guided reflection assignments, and created quality feedback activities for these assignments. However, the limitation to this study is simply that these tasks are artificial and often seen by students as unrealistic.

Speaking with my students majoring in education, I found agreement with much of the current research in that while they believe that exercises in unit and lesson plan development, assessment design, and reflection protocols are steps in the right direction and essential to teacher training, these tasks were not seen in classrooms that they observed (personal communication). As students fulfill practicum observations, they are not privy to the planning process, nor to the reflective process that the observed teacher goes through. Being given a few minutes to speak with the teacher about the lesson to be observed and to at least orally reflect on the lesson that they just observed would be beneficial. PTs look at the lesson plans and the lessons being taught by their CTs as complete elements and do not see the actual thought processes that go into the finished lesson design. The PT would have a more complete picture of the teaching process if CTs took the time to explain why a particular lesson was being taught, why it was being taught in a particular way, how the teacher felt that the lesson went, and how the teacher felt the lesson could be improved or changed. Therefore, explicitly training mentors to model reflection and to work directly with PTs on developing their reflective skills is critical.

Hudson, Usak, and Savron-Gencer (2009) suggest focused mentoring instruction, providing CTs with training on how to foster quality mentoring, and thus, purposeful reflection in the PTs they work with. They explore Hudson's (2007, as cited in Hudson, Usak, & Savron-Gencer, 2009) "five-factor model", which includes personal attributes, system requirements, pedagogical knowledge, modeling, and feedback, indicating that CTs need to be trained to walk a fine line between their dual role as "confidant and assessor" (p. 64). Other studies have examined the effects of collaborative training interventions between universities and school districts for the development of reflective practices among CTs. The assumptions used to design these professional development activities include that reflection is critical to helping PTs connect theory to practice and that PTs and CTs "must be involved in extensive activities about teaching and learning through self-inquiry and critical reflection" (Mitchel, 2007, p. 2). The results of extensive training actually fostered more reflective skills and strategies in the CTs as they became more focused on their task as mentors, in that they "had to self-reflect to have meaningful discussions with the novices in their charge" (p. 5). Another positive result of this collaborative training was that CTs were required to work with each other and developed what Farrell (2015) called "critical friendships", and reported that communicating with peers allowed them "to gain perspective on their challenges of teaching and to receive ideas from peers with whom they had developed bonds of trust" (p. 5).

This type of training is similar to the multidimensional mentoring model implemented among participants during my own Fulbright experience in Taiwan, where multiple levels of support were not only built into the teaching framework, but also multiple levels of dialogic journaling allowed the

Academic Advisor to communicate weekly with the experienced, Local English Teachers (LETs), and their native English speaking Fulbright English Teaching Assistants (ETAs) (Trites, Sroda, & Tseng, 2009). Within this framework, bi-monthly professional development workshops were held, a group of experienced teacher experts and the academic advisor observed the LETs and ETAs and provided feedback, and the academic advisor journaled weekly with each LET and ETA separately to discuss lesson planning and to reflect on lessons and other interpersonal, cross-cultural dynamics that occurred within the classroom. All participants felt that there was a strong support network in place and felt comfortable communicating not only their victories, but also their trials in the classroom.

With every positive approach, there are always drawbacks that need to be addressed. First, due to the siloed nature of teaching and the almost unbearable strain on CTs' time, peer mentoring and quality reflection fall by the wayside (Pomson, 2005; Schlichte, Yessel, & Marbler, 2005). Peer mentoring is risky, as it can be wrongly perceived as weakness and a call for help. This perspective needs to change. In addition, administrators need to realize that more reflective teachers are more purposeful in their instruction and allot more time for reflection, peer-to-peer mentoring, and CT/PT mentoring support, such as in a Professional Learning Community (PLC) specifically focused on reflective practices.

4   Personal Reflection: A Local Model

Based on my personal experience as a university supervisor (US), I have observed varying levels of preservice teachers' ability and willingness to reflect. It is not clear whether this variation is due to lack of training, time restrictions, or lack of willingness to engage. PTs at a midwestern regional university are required to complete a weekly professional growth plan (PGP) in which they are to select one goal for the week, list strategies or activities required to attain the goal, provide reasoning for the need to complete the strategies, document the date completed, and provide a brief reflection on the progress made toward the weekly goal. This PGP is signed by both the PT and CT. In addition, PTs are required to complete a weekly Reflection Report, which is not seen or signed by the CT, with the following tasks and questions:

1. Summarize your student teaching experience during the past week.
2. List two strengths of your teaching this week and how they contributed to your development as a teacher.
3. List the co-teaching strategies you used during this week for student teaching.

4. What impact have the co-teaching strategies had on student learning?
5. What impact has your instruction had on student learning? (Student Teaching Weekly Reflection).

These Reflection Reports, along with the PGP, Co-teaching Report, and Time Log, are sent to the US. Often, the PT is not familiar with the US, which can result in the PT feeling that they cannot be completely open in their reflections. Ideally, the PGP and the Reflection Report provide the opportunity for collaborative reflection; however, often the documents are exercises in futility. In one situation, the CT signed the PGP when it was still blank at the end of the week, allowing the PT to complete it at home, without feedback or collaboration. Another PT submitted very cursory PGPs, which were seen and signed by the CT, along with basic Reflection Reports every week. Even after being repeatedly advised by the US to be more reflective, the PT still submitted extremely similar weekly reflections that showed unwillingness to engage in the reflective process.

Based on these personal experiences, I developed a research study (approved through the University Institutional Review Board) that incorporated three different, but similar questionnaires to administer to three groups affiliated with a regional midwestern university in the United States: PTs, CTs, and USs during one semester. These surveys were created to inquire about each population's understanding of the importance of reflection, the practices of the PTs, and the role that the CTs and USs play in the preparation of the teacher candidates. One area of interest was how involved the CT was in the weekly PGP. In addition, questions asked about how often the CTs reflected on their own teaching practices and whether they modeled effective reflective practices for the PTs. Finally, each survey allowed participants to provide a personal response to each question if the traditional Likert scale was not reflective of their thoughts. In addition, they were provided with an open response section at the end of the survey to include any additional feedback that they would like to be included in the study. By agreeing to participate in the study and respond to the survey, all participants were assured of anonymity, as no identifying information was collected. In addition, by agreeing to participate, all participants knew that their responses would be analyzed and quoted.

4.1 *Pre-Service Teachers*

Surveys were sent to 67 PTs who were enrolled in the final practicum semester of their undergraduate program. These PTs are required to complete 70 days of student teaching, for which they are given the following assignments: weekly time sheets, weekly Professional Growth Plans (PGP), weekly Reflection Report, weekly Co-Teaching Report, four observed teaching lessons (one being part of a more developed unit plan), and a teaching portfolio. Of the 67 surveys that were emailed, only 16 PTs responded, for a return rate of 23.88%. Of these 16 PTs, 15 indicated that they were 20–25 years of age and were female, while one preferred not to answer.

4.2 Cooperating Teachers

A similar survey was sent to 130 CTs. These teachers must have a minimum of 3 years of teaching in the certified field, are required to undergo training to qualify as CTs, and are compensated for their participation in that capacity. Of the 130 surveys emailed to the CTs, 46 were returned, for a return rate of 35.38%. Of the 46 CTs, 42 were female and 4 male, with ages ranging from 26 to over 65 and the majority CTs being between 31 and 40 years of age. These CTs reported approximately 11–15 years of teaching experience on average, with the lowest being 3–5 years (the minimum required for serving as a CT) and the highest being over 30 years. When it came to the number of years serving as a CT, a very even split with the number of years of experience was reported, as shown in Table 3.1.

TABLE 3.1 Years of experience as a cooperating teacher

Number of years as CT	Number of CTs reporting
1–3	15
4–6	9
7–9	7
10+	15

4.3 University Supervisors

A third survey, similar to the other two, was sent to 23 USs, a group of teachers who currently hold a variety of positions. Some are faculty within the university, and others are retired teachers and administrators who are hired for this task. As USs, they are required to attend a training session at the beginning of each semester, for which they are assigned at least one teacher candidate. They meet with the CT and PT to ensure that all involved understand the guidelines set up by the university, receive and respond to all of the PTs' weekly reports, grade their portfolio, and observe them in action. Of the 23 surveys emailed, only 11 were returned. This return rate of 47.82% was greater than those of the other two groups. Of the USs, 10 were female and 1 male, with ages ranging from 31 to over 65, and 5 of the 11 reporting being over 65. All 11 USs have served as public school teachers, and 6 of the 11 have served as CTs previously, as shown in Table 3.2.

TABLE 3.2 University supervisor experiences

Varied experience	1–3 Years	4–6 Years	7–9 Years	10+ Years	Total
Also served as a cooperating teacher	2	1	0	3	6
Year as university supervisor	6	0	3	2	11

4.4 Results

While the return rate for each of the surveys was low, the homogeneity of responses provides at least some direction for analysis and discussion. Most of the respondents stated the importance of reflection and mentoring, yet the design of the reflective assignments was brought into question.

PTs were consistent in their view that reflective practices were beneficial and that they felt that the CTs modeled reflective practices. The largest area of variance was in the amount of time PTs reported spending on completing their weekly PGPs and Reflection Reports, with some commenting that they spent a considerable amount of time completing these reports, while others reported spending a minimal amount of time. Related to this finding was that some PTs reported that they often wrote the same thing in their weekly PGPs. While most scores were high (4/5 – agree/strongly agree), the mean scores were similar – 2.63 (amount of time spent completing a report) and 2.81 (reported writing the same thing each week). When examining the individual scores, inverse reporting was found, which means that if they reported that they did not spend a great deal of time writing their PGPs, they also reported that they often wrote the same thing on their PGPs, and vice-versa. Of those who reported a negative view of the PGPs, they also reported that they found this activity a "complete waste of time", while the other PTs reported the complete opposite. Individual statements from a few PTs indicated that while they felt reflection was important, they also felt that the mechanisms put in place were not conducive to effective reflection. In addition, they indicated that the weekly reporting took up a considerable amount of time that could be better spent on lesson planning and collaborating with their CT. One PT stated it this way:

> While I understand that these forms are important for you all to know we are completing our student teaching to the best of our ability, asking brand new teachers to complete a two-page reflection report, a one-page co-teaching report, a co-teaching lesson planning sheet, and hours [reporting the number of field hours] is quite a bit to add on top of our regular lesson planning, grading, and participation in any required extra-curricular activities. I spend several hours each week completing forms

for you all to look at in order to see if you believe I'm doing a good job. I believe that this time could be better spent developing student-centered lessons and providing feedback on my students' completed work.

Another PT concurred, stating:

> I feel as if all of the information that we must provide in the binder is busy work, and a complete waste of time .... I also believe that the weekly growth plan is a good strategy, but I believe that it takes up too much [time] when there is already a lot of other stuff that we have to do for student teaching.

CTs mostly reported that reflection was good and that the weekly reports were beneficial. Only one CT consistently disagreed with this statement. When it came to the effective use of time and unique reporting on the PGPs, there was greater variability. When CTs provided written comments, they indicated that they felt that weekly reports might be too much and that the conversations between the PT and CT were more important that the written report. When asked if they modeled reflective teaching practices for their PTs, all but one CT reported that they felt that they did this effectively. When asked if they could do a better job modeling reflective practices, there was greater variability. One CT stated:

> Although I reflect daily on my teaching practices, I don't do it in written form. My student teachers and I always discuss these things, but spending time writing down the reflection can sometimes seem like a waste of precious time that could be spent grading, preparing lessons, and discussing teaching practices. I understand the need for documentation, but good teachers reflect constantly without having to write it down.

The USs had a very strong, almost visceral, reaction to the importance of reflection and the effectiveness of the PTs' ability to reflect. All of the USs reported that they regularly reflect on their teaching practices, and all but one strongly agreed that reflection is a critical component of professional development. Consistently, the USs felt that the PTs and CTs were taking the role of reflection and mentoring seriously. The only two questions that showed considerable variability were the same as for the CTs: Whether the PGPs were a waste of time and whether the PTs wrote the same thing each week on their PGPs. One US indicated that she felt that three PGPs a term would be sufficient and that the PTs possibly wrote the same thing week to week "because they do not have the PD to attend nor understand what is happening". When giving general reflections, one US stated:

> I believe that, if not required, student teachers would not pause to reflect on these necessary elements of their student teaching experience. Most student teacher candidates feel stressed to complete the necessary requirements; therefore, reflections might fall to the wayside, if not required. Because of the requirement, the teacher candidate will hopefully realize the importance of regular reflection during his/her teaching career.

5   Next Steps for Mentoring Reflection

Based on the findings of this study, it is clear that teachers and future teachers see the value of reflection; however, the results of the survey study indicate that many do not feel the need to reflect in writing. Both PTs and CTs, and even some USs, in the study reported that taking the extra time to reflect in writing took away valuable time that could be better spent with other related tasks. Based on the research, though, it is possible that even though the PTs stated that the CTs reflected on their own teaching practices, it was unclear that the PTs were able to learn by example, and it is possible that they need more explicit instruction. While research has shown that students find the practice activities to be cumbersome and somewhat unrealistic, it becomes important to model reflection more explicitly, which means that we as educators need to do a better job articulating our own reflections to our students in the pre-service classroom, and that CTs must be trained to overtly model reflection. In addition, while reflection reports are an effective way to communicate to the USs, who are not in the classroom every day, these could be redesigned to be more dialogic and to ask more focused questions on not only what happened during the past week, but also why certain decisions were made. Thus, the problem with poor reflective practices in PTs is four-fold:

1. PTs do not know how to reflect purposefully.
2. PTs are not aware that they are actually seeing reflection being modeled.
3. CTs may reflect, but do not do so in a manner that is clearly evident to the PTs.
4. CTs are not trained to foster reflection.

First, a couple of assumptions must be made for CTs to begin mentoring reflection: They need to understand that they are not only responsible for mentoring and supervising PTs in their teaching, but also in their reflection; and that neither reflection nor mentoring is intuitive or solitary. Based on these assumptions, it is critical that CTs and USs are trained to more explicitly model and mentor reflection in the classroom. In addition, a mentoring program that is reciprocal among the PT, CT, and US is important. In this local situation, both the CT and the US undergo minimal training, yet do not interact with each other until the US visits the CT and PT in the classroom. A first step would be to have all CTs and USs participate in a training session where more information about the need for critical reflection is shared.

In pre-service classrooms, adding direct instruction on reflective practices instead of simply including reflective assignments for the students would be helpful. Helping these students understand the varying purposes for reflection and how that reflection can be beneficial to their professional development will serve them better when they are actually completing their various field experiences.

Another change would be to modify the questions asked of the PTs in their weekly reflections, focusing on questions of *why* and *how* instead of *what*. By doing this, they would begin to dig deeper into the teaching process and make connections between their personal beliefs and theories, both pedagogical and content (Farrell, 2019; Quirke & Allison, 2008, 2010; Quirke, this volume). In addition, the reflection should be changed from a weekly report to a dialogue journal, which would allow for more personal interaction to take place. Since PTs often report on what happened from day to day, guided reflection questions in this reflective journal could include the following:

1. What specific events happened this week that went well?
2. Why do you think they were successful?
3. What events didn't go well?
4. Why do you think they didn't go well? Are there things that you did that could have contributed to the negative situation?
5. What would you do the same or differently to improve both the positive and negative experiences?
6. Why would you select this new strategy? How do these strategies connect with your training?
7. What lessons will you take away from your experiences this week that will help you in the future?
8. What do you believe that the CT and/or US can do to help you as you develop as a teacher?

Note that these questions ask the preservice teacher to not only reflect on *WHAT* went well or poorly, but on *WHY* they think it did. This additional question of *WHY* will help instill true reflection, as opposed to simply reporting.

Second, during CT training, the inclusion of mentoring training is critical, instructing CTs to be more explicit with their planning *and* reflecting. Also, requiring the CT to work with the PT to complete this reflection would actually foster pedagogical instruction. To ensure that the CTs do work with the PTs on this task, a short reflective dialogue journal could be maintained between the CT and the US to allow for more interaction and accountability. The CTs could be asked many of the same, or similar, questions as in the PT dialogue journal. While this may appear to be putting more work on the CT, it does allow for more transparency and accountability and helps ensure that they are doing their part to be reflective. If these journals are similar, it would encourage the PT and CT to communicate more effectively. CTs should be taught to overtly reflect on their teaching with the PT; once the PT takes over instruction, the PT and CT should take the time to do mini reflective activities after the lessons. This change would create a multidirectional dialogue, where all involved in the PT's practicum would be communicating more frequently and with more meaning (see Figure 3.1).

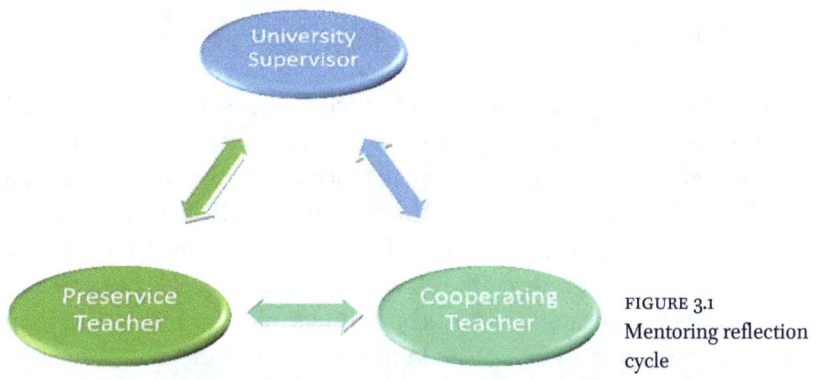

FIGURE 3.1
Mentoring reflection cycle

Third, when the US observes the PT, the post-observation session should begin with a moment of PT self-reflection, similar to that between the daily CT and PT. Questions such as the following could be developed:
1. How do you feel that your lesson went? (Provide an example or two if possible.)
2. Why do you think it went well or not?
3. How effective do you think your interactions with your students were? (Examples)
4. Why do you think these interactions were successful or not?
5. What do you think you could do to improve them?
6. Why do you think these changes could be effective?

7. What lessons will you take away from this observation to help you in the future?

After this short, guided reflection, the US could then provide their own observations and suggestions. If time and scheduling allow, having a group discussion among the PT, CT, and US would be very beneficial, because it would allow the PT to participate in peer-to-peer reflection.

While these are small changes from what takes place every day in the classroom, the change from a static report format to a more dialogic framework would allow for open discussion and more reflection. CTs are selected because of their expertise and dedication to teaching. Since they get little compensation for the work that they do, it is clear that they take their role as a mentor and trainer seriously; therefore, bringing mentoring and reflection to the forefront would help CTs focus more of their own time on reflective practices. These activities would foster a productive mentoring environment, centered upon reflective planning and collaboration.

6 Conclusion

As is evident through myriad research studies and the current research reported here, PTs, while well-intentioned, often do not have the requisite skills to provide quality reflection on their teaching practices. It, therefore, becomes the responsibility of the CTs and USs to be more explicit in their mentoring and training of the PTs, actually articulating the reflective steps that they take as they plan, instruct, and assess daily. Following the many models presented in this chapter, these educators, and teacher leaders, need to model reflective practice in a more purposeful way and include the PT in thoughtful collaborative discussions of effective teaching practices. CTs and USs, being selected because of their skill in and passion for teaching, should be provided with more detailed mentoring and leadership training on how to best mentor the PTs they work with. In addition, collaborative reflection among the PTs, CTs, and USs would develop a multi-dimensional reflective support network that will benefit not only these educators, but also the students in their classes.

References

Azizah, U. A., Nurkanto, J., & Drajati, N. A. (2018). Reflective practice: The experiences of preservice EFL teachers in teaching English. *Journal of Language and Linguistic Studies, 14*(3), 133–144.

Brandt, C. (2008). Integrating feedback and reflection in teacher preparation. *ELT Journal, 62*(1), 37–46. doi:10.1093/elt/ccm076

Ciavaldini-Cartaut, S. (2015). Moving beyond the reflectivity of post-lesson mentoring conferences in teacher education and creating learning/development opportunities for pre-service teachers. *European Journal of Teacher Education, 38,* 496–511. http://dx.doi.org/10.1080/02619768.2015.1056909

College of Education and Human Services Teacher Education Services. (2019). *Cooperating teacher information: Guiding the teacher candidate.* Murray State University, Murray, KY.

Farrell, T. S. C. (2013). *Reflective teaching* (ELT Development Series). Teachers of English to Speakers of Other Languages.

Farrell, T. S. C. (2015). *Language teacher professional development* (ELT Development Series). Teachers of English to Speakers of Other Languages.

Farrell, T. S. C. (2019). *Reflection-as-action* (ELT Development Series). Teachers of English to Speakers of Other Languages.

Frick, L., Carl, A., & Beets, P. (2010). Reflection as learning about the self in context: Mentoring as catalyst for reflective development in pre-service teachers. *South African Journal of Education, 30,* 421–437.

Ganser, T. (2002). How teachers compare the roles of cooperating teacher and mentor. *The Educational Forum, 66,* 380–385.

Hudson, P., Nguyen, H. T. M., & Hudson, S. (2009). Mentoring EFL preservice teachers in EFL writing. *TESOL Canada Journal, 27*(1), 85–102.

Hudson, P., Usak, M., & Savran-Gancer, A. (2009). Employing the five-factor mentoring instrument: Analyzing mentoring practices for teaching primary science. *European Journal of Teacher Education, 32*(1), 63–74. doi:10.1080/02619760802509115

Jones, J., & Jones, K. (2013). Teaching reflective practice: Implementation in the teacher-education setting. *The Teacher Educator, 48,* 73–85. doi:10.1080/08878730.202.740153

Lakshmi, D. S. (2009). Journal writing: A means of professional development in ESL classrooms at undergraduate level. *Journal of Language and Linguistic Studies, 5*(2), 9–20.

Lee, I. (2007). Preparing pre-service English teachers for reflective practice. *ELT Journal, 61,* 321–329. doi:10.1093/elt/ccm022

Mauri, T., Clarà, M., Colomina, R., & Onrubia, J. (2016). Educational assistance to improve reflective practice among student teachers. *Electronic Journal of Research in Educational Psychology, 14*(2), 287–309.

Middleton, M., Abrams, E., & Seamon, J. (2011). Resistance and deintensification in reflective practice with preservice teaching interns. *New Directions for Teaching & Learning, 126,* 67–75. doi:10:1002/tl.445

Mitchel, L. Z. (2007). Locating reflective practices: Finding from a self-study. *Networks, 10*(1), 1–9.

Peyton, J. K. (2009). Building an international community of scholars and practitioners through e-mail journaling. In J. Burton, P. Quirke, C. Reichmann, & J. K. Peyton (Eds.), *Reflective writing: A way to lifelong teacher learning*. TESL-EJ online journal (pp. 156–165). http://tesl-ej.org/books/reflective_writing.pdf

Pomson, A. D. M. (2005). One classroom at a time? Teacher isolation and community viewed through the prism of the particular. *Teachers College Record, 107*, 783–802.

Quirke, P. (2011). Developing the foundation for DREAM management. In C. Coombe, L. Stephenson, & S. Abu-Rmaileh (Eds.), *Leadership and management in English language teaching* (pp. 67–79). TESOL Arabia.

Quirke, P., & Allison, S. (2008). DREAM management: Involving and motivating teachers. In C. Coombe (Ed.), *Leadership in English language teaching and learning* (pp. 186–201). University of Michigan Press.

Quirke, P., & Allison, S. (2010). Building leaders through mentoring. In J. A. Carmona (Ed.), *Language teaching and learning in ESL education: Current issues, collaborations and practice. Leadership skills for English language educators* (pp. 179–192). Kona Publishing.

Richards, J., & Lockhart, C. (1994). *Reflective teaching in second language classrooms*. Cambridge University Press.

Schlichte, J., Yessel, N., & Marbler, J. (2005). Pathways to burnout: Case studies in teacher isolation and alienation. *Preventing School Failure, 50*(1), 35–41.

Sempowicz, T., & Hudson, P. (2012). Mentoring pre-service teachers' reflective practices towards producing teaching outcomes. *Journal of Evidence Based Coaching and Mentoring, 10*(2), 52–64.

Töman, U. (2017). Investigation of reflective teaching practice effect on training development skills of the preservice teachers. *Journal of Education and Training Studies, 5*(6), 232–239. https://doi.org/10.11114/jets.v5i6.2348

Trites, L., Sroda, M. S., & Tseng, J. M. (2009). *Multi-dimensional co-teaching/mentoring model for on-the-job teacher training*. Unpublished manuscript.

Wlodarsky, R. (2018). The benefits of reflection on improving teaching through change: A reflective model for professional development. *National Teacher Education Journal, 11*(1), 33–41.

CHAPTER 4

Co-Leadership through Dialogue and Reflective Writing in the Teaching Practicum

Carla Reichmann

Language teacher supervision in the 21st century presents us with myriad contexts that challenge us constantly as teacher educators, with new student teachers, novel life stories, new texts to consider, and diverse schools. Addressing an internship supervision experience in 2019, this chapter focuses on student teacher writing and co-leadership development, triggered by dialogue and reflective practices in the practicum at the Modern Letters undergraduate program at a Brazilian public university. The practicum included field work at the Adalgisa Cunha Institute for the Blind in Paraíba (henceforth ICPAC, the Brazilian acronym).

In line with Freire (1996), it is significant to point out that "the best way a teacher can take care of his or her authority is to respect the freedom of the students" (p. 164). Just for the record: Paulo Freire is from the Brazilian northeast, where he worked, taught, and developed his unique adult literacy praxis defending problem-posing, progressive education, and critical pedagogy (Freire, 1970). With the current polarization and geopolitical and ecological instability that many of us are facing worldwide, Freire's perspective is as relevant as ever, especially in the realm of quality public education.

This chapter aims to shed light on a co-leadership relationship in the English as a Foreign Language (EFL) teaching practicum, giving student teachers a voice, identity, and leadership opportunities, as portrayed in their reflective internship reports. Besides the unique context involving blind language learners, another significant aspect of the practicum concerns shared leadership between the cooperating teacher and the university supervisor. The student teachers (henceforth STs) textualized their practicum experiences in a twofold manner, interacting with the cooperating teacher, and with the university supervisor, in different ways.

> Leadership, according to the DREAM educational perspective, can be defined as placing teachers at the core of the educational enterprise as those closest to the students who are the raison d'être for us all. Therefore, effective educational leadership should *create and maintain an*

environment conducive to collaborative learning with and for students. It focuses on 'observables' in teaching – space, time, learning and teaching activities, communication, interaction, atmosphere, and artifacts. It also highlights 'unobservables': the individual affective, social psychological factors; cognitive domain factors; group factors; and wider social, cultural, and other influences. (Quirke, 2014, p. 2; Chapter 2, this volume)

On analyzing teacher triad dynamics in internships, Benites et al. (2015) point out that the university supervisor is expected to lead. On the same note, regarding collaboration between cooperating teachers and university supervisors, Portelance et al. (2016) raise the same issue, that "leadership is expected from the university supervisor", and question "whether supervisors make enough room for co-trainers [...]" (p. 47). These are definitely relevant points, and my response would be yes, university supervisors in the teaching practicum can make room for cooperating teachers, and forge more symmetrical co-leader relationships. According to Benites et al. (2015, p. 106),

> [m]ore specifically, in the Brazilian context, the figure of the cooperating teacher is still imprecise. As mentioned previously, the internship model adopted in the country presents various fragilities, especially in terms of school-university relations (Souza Neto, Sarti, & Benites, 2011). These relations, when established, are often based on comradeship between university professors and collaborators at schools. (All translations in this chapter are those of the author.)

These observations hold true in the context described in this chapter. Unforeseen personal, institutional, academic, and bureaucratic factors can occur each academic semester in regards to the practicum, creating tension and uncertainty in the process. Yes, the internship model is a rather fragile construct, taking into account many aspects that involve students in transit between different educational institutions, schools, and universities, as well as taking into account the lack of clarity regarding the cooperating teacher's role in Brazil. Comradeship does play an important role, as discussed below.

Okech (2008, p. 237) explains that "[c]o-leadership is the practice of leading a group in collaboration with another counselor with the objective of facilitating therapeutic or group interaction for group members" (Yalom & Leszcz, 2005). Along these lines, this EFL practicum functioned in a parallel manner, in that two supervisors were collaborating with the objective of facilitating teacher development and interaction among group members.

In sum, this chapter discusses the vital importance of dialogue, reflective writing, and co-leadership development in a learning community, and by means of 16 selected fragments extracted from internship reports, explores the role of the cooperating teacher as a co-leader in the practicum.

The following sections address core concepts: the macro and microcontexts for the practicum and the cooperating teacher-university supervisor relationship. The chapter closes with reflections on the patterns found and the changes in the teachers that became evident to them and to me during the practicum.

1 Core Concepts

According to Bailey, Burkett, and Freeman (2008), "classrooms are, first and foremost, language environments" (p. 608). In line with this concept, some underlying assumptions that ground the research that provides the basis for this chapter are described briefly here, addressing the role of dialogue in learning, the New Literacy Studies, and Labor Sciences.

Bakhtin (2000), as part of his work on discursive genres, offers a sociocultural perspective of language relevant to this study. He explains that "language penetrates life by means of concrete utterances, and it is also by means of concrete utterances that life penetrates language" (p. 282). Visualizing the complex social fabric that sustains social voice, Bakhtin explains that "each utterance is a link in a very complex chain of other utterances" (p. 291), and real dialogue is the simplest and most classical form of verbal interaction. Dialogue is also construed by means of other spheres of verbal communication, constituted by complex, layered dialogic responses.

Taking the importance of dialogue into account, the following parallel can be drawn with the literacy practices in the practicum, in that the verbal flux in which student teachers are immersed in our classes involves various chains of utterances; over time, student teacher narratives (oral and written texts) can document teacher identity development by signaling construction of socioprofessional voice.

Kleiman's (1995) perspective on language teacher education and literacy practices stems from Freirean and Bakhtinian perspectives, grounded in the New Literacies Studies Group (Barton et al., 2000; Street, 2003; among others). Situated in the field of Applied Linguistics, Kleiman's work has had a strong impact in Brazilian education and has influenced my perspective on the supervised internship as a socioprofessional literacy practice (Kleiman& Reichmann, 2012; Reichmann, 2015). According to Barton and Hamilton (2000), *"literacy is best understood as a set of social practices; these are observable in events which are mediated by texts"* (p. 9, original emphasis). The scholars clarify that on "encompassing what people do with texts and what these activities mean to them, [... and] how texts fit into the practices of people's lives, rather than the other way around" (p. 9), literacy events encapsulate a basic concept in this perspective, involving

> activities where literacy has a role. Usually there is a written text, or texts, central to the activity and there may be talk around the text. Events are observable episodes which arise from practices and are shaped by them. The notion of events stresses the situated nature of literacy, that it always exists in a social context. (p. 8)

In other words, social practices generate literacy events, triggering written and spoken texts. Along these lines, based on various social practices, STS can verbalize their experiences – orally or in writing – promoted by the literacy events organized by the cooperating teacher and the university supervisor.

Machado's publication, *Teaching as Work: A Discursive Approach* (2004), opened a new line of educational/Applied Linguistics inquiry in Brazil, drawing on Sociodiscursive Interactionism (Bronckart, 1999) and the Labor Sciences. For the purposes of this chapter, I would like to specifically mention two researchers in the field of Labor Sciences, René Amigues and Yves Clot. In regards to the teacher's role, Amigues (2004) explains that "for the teacher, *class management* implies construing collective dimensions for individual action, and having *a class that works* means not only having good students, but rather a cohesive collective forged and ready to engage in action [...]" (p. 48). This definition is significantly in line with the DREAM leadership perspective described in Chapter 2, in the sense that effective educational leadership can develop by placing teachers at the core of the process, forging cohesive collectives, that can make the class work.

Clot (2007), based on Vygotsky's and Bakthin's work, envisioned the concept of 'real work', all of the activities that a professional has planned and visualized for a given work day, *but the activities do not happen,* for whatever reason. These unrealized activities are invisible unless the professional has opportunities to talk about them. In regards to teaching, for example, real work includes all of the unobservables in a given class that could have hindered the activities in the lesson plan. These unobservables can only be grasped when talking to the teacher in question – something the four STS always had a chance to do with their cooperating teacher.

Based on Clot's concept of real work, 'the iceberg metaphor' (Medrado, 2012, p. 156) has been an invaluable image with our student teachers, whereby the visible teaching aspects are represented by the ice block above the water, and the invisible aspects of teaching are underwater, submerged. In class discussions with the STS, the iceberg metaphor is often invoked, and the STS often mention the iceberg in class as well as in their internship reports, disclosing unobservables in their teaching. In sum, teaching is a situated activity, and the unpredictability of classrooms can be a major stress factor for student teachers. Problematizing this issue can open student teachers' eyes to the fact that unpredictable situations are recurrent and lesson plans are not cast in stone, but rather the opposite holds true: flexibility is crucial, for teaching plans are unstable and fluctuate. The next section addresses general and local contexts for the supervised internship at ICPAC (Adalgisa Cunha Institute for the Blind in Paraíba).

2   The Practicum: Macro and Microcontexts

According to Brazilian teacher licensing criteria, and in order to comply with the national legal system, the supervised internship in Brazil follows a series of federal laws, such as those set forth by the Education National Council (Brasil, 2002a, 2002b) and the National Curricular Guidelines (Brasil, 2015), which determine parameters for university curricula and the practicum. Following these directions, the supervised internship must happen in the second half of the undergraduate program, encompasses 400 hours, and each institution of higher education can organize these hours as they deem necessary (in general, the format has been four 100-hour modules, over two years).

Another relevant national resolution is Law# 11.788 (Brasil, 2008), popularly known as 'the Internship Law'. According to this law, the following features were established: student teachers must devise an internship activities plan in their internship commitment term; the maximum weekly workload must be clearly defined in the curriculum; the curricular and non-curricular supervised internship must be included in the program's pedagogical project; student teachers must have institutional coverage for accidents; and the cooperating institution and the university must assign teacher supervisors.

At the local level, the internship also has to abide by university and departmental regulations, which establish more situated parameters for curricula and internships. To say the least, a considerable number of institutional forms need to be provided to make the internship 'official' in the field and to ensure that undergraduate students are officially registered as student teachers in the online university platform.

On a personal level, in 2007, a new curriculum was implemented in the Modern Foreign Languages Department at the federal university where I have worked since 2004, which involved finally transferring the EFL supervised internship from the Education Department to our department. Previously, the Education Department was responsible for the teaching practicum; currently, Education is responsible for the elementary school practicum, and the undergraduate program is responsible for the middle and high school practicums. Actively involved in this process, facing this professional challenge as an internship supervisor was definitely another step for me as a teacher educator, stemming from previous teacher supervision experience as an English Language Fellow, at five binational centers in Bolivia and Brazil, and as a teacher researcher for my doctoral project, focusing on teacher development through dialogue journaling (Reichmann, 2001).

Therefore, in 2007, I formed a small group of professors that set in motion the curricular supervised internship in our department, opening a new front for those of us immersed in teacher education research projects, and involving action research in our own EFL practicums. Since then, the 'internship curricular axis' has constituted the backbone for my academic experiences, opening up many schools and relationships with teachers and grounding my teaching, advising, and research activities. Situated in the fields of Education and Applied Linguistics, and framed by qualitative research, my research projects focus on teacher development, reflective writing, social voice, and the practicum as a socioprofessional literacy practice.

Narrowing the context to the internship site, ICPAC is an institution focusing on education for the blind, established in 1944 in the capital city of Paraíba, João Pessoa. Initially a state-run institution, an NGO-state partnership is currently responsible for its functioning. Besides getting much-needed Braille literacy classes at ICPAC, visually impaired learners can socialize and engage in extracurricular activities with educational, psychological, and medical support, creating a vital supportive community. Programs are offered to school-age learners, and adult education classes are also offered. Learners have access to a computer lab, library, music classes, and sports facilities, among other spaces. Impressive trophy shelves can be seen in the gym: the ICPAC athletes are goalball and swimming champions, traveling internationally. All in all, learners can develop life skills, immersed in various social activities. It goes without saying that ICPAC is a second home for the visually impaired.

3 The Cooperating Teacher and University Supervisor Relationship

First and foremost, as suggested earlier, comradeship can play an important role in the school-university relations that frame the practicum. In this particular case, it is relevant to describe how the cooperating teacher (Rachel, a pseudonym) and the university professor (myself) construed dialogue and comradeship, which later enabled the emergence of co-leadership in the practicum.

My department's partnership with ICPAC stems from an inclusive education research project initiated by Dr. Betânia Medrado (2014), who volunteered as an EFL teacher at ICPAC in 2012, together with Rachel, then her advisee. Specific articles drawing from this project often inspire our undergraduate students. A volunteer teacher as well, Rachel became solely responsible for the EFL groups a few years later. By then, as a more experienced university supervisor, I had become extremely interested in this possible internship site for the STS. The necessary institutional agreement for ICPAC as an internship site was finally confirmed in 2016, and the EFL practicum at ICPAC immediately became a reality. Since then, Rachel and I have collaborated, and STS have had this potential site for their field work.

Rachel had been my undergraduate student years before, and I later followed her involvement with Medrado's inclusive education project. Initially aiming to become a translator, Rachel found herself as a teacher in the field of education for the blind. Under Medrado's advising in the Modern Letters undergraduate program, and later in the Linguistics graduate program, Rachel produced her final undergraduate paper, her MA thesis, and her PhD dissertation, strengthening her teacher researcher identity. I had participated in Rachel's undergraduate defense panel and attended her MA and PhD defenses. More recently, Rachel held a substitute teacher position in our department, and we ran into each other constantly on campus, creating more opportunities for dialogue.

My first visit to ICPAC happened in 2016, when Rachel and I were able to set up the four-month supervised internship. At ICPAC, under Rachel's sensitive and sensible guidance, I have seen STS thrive and flourish in a nurturing, nevertheless demanding, educational environment. STS at ICPAC learn to 'see' in different ways, due to the enriching life experiences and positive interactions with blind learners in class. STS engage in participant observation, and prodded by Rachel, soon take part in class activities, learn the basics of Braille, and produce and adapt specific learning materials and resources. Materials production with recycled objects is a fascinating aspect of Rachel's work (Medrado & Dantas, 2019).

Through the years, I could see Rachel expand her role as a cooperating teacher, triggering a very supportive framework for STS, in dialogue with the university. In other words, our comradeship evolved, strengthened, and matured, increasing learning opportunities for the undergraduate students.

My understanding is that by means of teacher literacy events, at the university as well as in the field, co-leadership enhanced teacher voice and triggered teacher identity construction.

In the next section, I describe the practicum experience through such events, grounded on 16 fragments extracted from reflective internship reports produced by four STs – Amy, Pat, Tina, and Vera (pseudonyms; permission has been granted by the four STs to publish these fragments, originally in Portuguese).

4   Co-Leadership in the Practicum

The participants were my own students at a public university, co-supervised by the cooperating teacher and me, so I can elaborate here on the student teachers' perceptions of the practicum experience as inscribed in the verbal flux of the practicum, whether orally, in class, or in writing. In this internship, as previously mentioned, the cooperating teacher increasingly collaborated with the university supervisor, sustaining the group members in our learning communities and facilitating teacher development. Thus the student teachers had two co-supervisors in action, one in the field and another one at the university, with diverse angles discussed in each context, contributing to an expanded verbal flow, more conducive to ST development.

In the second semester of 2019, I was assigned an undergraduate evening course focusing on the middle school practicum. On the first day, I presented a general overview of the course plan – readings, seminar, observation and teaching processes, relationship with the cooperating teacher, and possible sites for field work. I listed all of the schools, as usual, and asked who was free on Tuesday afternoons, when the EFL classes were held at ICPAC, with Rachel. Based on past internships there, I could honestly inform the STs that Rachel loves working collectively in the practicum and that they would have an unforgettable learning experience. Out of approximately 15 students, four adventurous young women promptly signed up: for Tina and Vera this would be their first classroom teaching experience, while Amy and Pat had prior EFL teaching experience in extension programs. They were also informed that the maximum number of blind learners in class is usually eight.

Our weekly classes at the university initially consisted of seminars and discussions and, once the students entered the field, observation notes and experiences were shared, forming a tight learning community. Regarding this supportive network, as Tina points out in her report, "The interaction between students and professor, in this phase of the course, is doubtless a source of reflection and encouragement …".

I often remind students how they are gradually constructing their final reflective internship reports with their oral and written texts produced during the semester. I convey to students that the common ground for their final report is the shared verbal flux surrounding us throughout the practicum, and I also stress that as a reader, my expectation is that their final reports 'continue' our dialogue: the report is yet another response within our verbal flux, a Bakhtinian response, in dialogue with the social voices and texts echoing in the practicum.

On entering the field, Amy, Pat, Tina, and Vera returned with thought-provoking narratives about their first visit at ICPAC and with positive feelings regarding the cooperating teacher, as stated below:

Fragment 1
The cooperating teacher was receptive and made us feel at ease during the first visit, clarifying doubts and suggesting readings, while she introduced us to employees and learners we met on the way. (Tina)

On this first visit, the STs meet the cooperating teacher, tour the institution, and take their official presentation letter. Rachel's receptivity is a crucial affective factor, constantly mediating interactions. At the university, these STs, in particular, addressed many questions from other STs regarding the context and, as in many internships, unpredictable episodes often arose, triggering much discussion and reflection in class.

Before they actually met the blind learners in the classroom, however, this semester Rachel had added another activity, exploring mobile phone resources:

Fragment 2
An initial highlight was the learner audios we received from the teacher after the visit, where the learners revealed their expectations in this process. Classroom themes, patience, timing for classroom interaction, and as much as possible wait time were needed for the learners to develop whatever was solicited. (Tina)

The audios visibly triggered a wave of excitement, and the four STs became aware, right away, of the extra time that these learners needed to process classroom activities, a challenge constantly mentioned in their reports. Rachel soon introduced the STs to Braille and the writing equipment, and the materials she brought to class were a major source of amazement and inspiration. Rachel gradually shared with the STs another perspective on classroom life, how to respond when learners cannot see. Thus, many educational and literacy practices have to be adapted. STs become aware that the main changes one has to adopt regarding teacher interaction with blind learners involve the longer time needed for activities to be successful and the need for more physical closeness. The scarcity of teaching materials for the blind is another major challenge. Importantly, Rachel deconstructed misconceptions and stereotypes associated with blindness.

Insecurity regarding teaching and the teaching context was gently addressed by the cooperating teacher, soon triggering interactions between the STs and the blind learners focused on establishing a secure environment and promoting empathy, trust, and bonding. Expanding her supervision responsibilities, co-planning was another innovative strategy that Rachel adopted with the STs (with excellent results), as can be seen below:

> *Fragment 3*
> For the first planning session, the teacher suggested a reading, *Three Days to See*, by the U.S. writer and inclusion activist, Helen Keller (1933). While reading the text, I associated it to the movie scenes in *The Miracle Worker* (1962) … (Tina)

> *Fragment 4*
> In this initial meeting, July 3, we planned a didactic sequence focusing on sports, a topic which is very present in learners' lives at the Institute. Teacher Rachel revealed to be an extremely competent and caring teacher … she patiently explained to us details about the practicum and the learners, and suggested further readings and materials in Braille […] Besides this, she encouraged us to feed a scrapbook [author's note. a digital portfolio] on a weekly basis, sending us the template by email on the same day, so we could communicate our perceptions, discoveries and difficulties during the practicum, and she would read our notes and comment on a weekly basis too. (Pat)

Besides planning together, the above-mentioned scrapbook was an additional tool that the cooperating teacher adopted, consisting of PowerPoint templates that the STs produced after each classroom experience and which they shared at the university, often with many pictures, emojis, and written texts.

In this first planning session, the STs quickly realized the relevance of sports in the ICPAC community and focused on sports and fair play as a learning theme. They met the Physical Education teacher/goalball trainer, became familiar with the game, and planned an out-of-class activity for the following week, after attending their first EFL class. Thus they went to a goalball training session, and when they shared this afterwards, at the university, their amazement was visible, and an emotional narrative ensued. A revealing excerpt follows:

> *Fragment 5*
> On the same day, in the evening, we saw the goalball team training, and the athletes we saw in action were simply incredible. The game is very exciting, and as all players are blind or blindfolded [due to low vision], they need silence in order to hear the bells jingling inside the ball, so that they know where the ball is during the game. Even though we were aware of the need for silence, we could barely contain our enthusiasm with their exemplary game and perfectly executed strategies. We had to constantly contain our yelling and clapping, sometimes unsuccessfully. It's interesting that all the instructions for the official game are given in English, showing an evident relationship between sports and language. At a certain point, the trainer asked us, one by one, to give instructions for a few minutes, which made us quite nervous. At the end, all went well. (Pat)

As Pat mentions above, since the oral instructions for the game are in English, the trainer asked the STs to actually participate in the game and interact with the players, forging yet another rich internship experience. As for the sports theme, this soon triggered much planning and involved materials production, namely, medals. This class activity at ICPAC triggered much discussion in our learning community at the university, especially regarding some unpredictable situations with the medals, as can be seen below:

> *Fragment 6*
> In order to win a medal, the learners had to recognize the sounds related to some sports (such as swimming, soccer and goalball), and relate them to the previously taught sports vocabulary. (Tina)

> *Fragment 7*
> In general, the activity was very successful: everyone was engaged, focused and all participated. Our group produced medals with the words gold, silver and bronze in ink and in Braille, as a reward for the winners in the competition. Then things got a bit complicated, for not all learners were satisfied with the manner in which the competition developed, and with the results. (Pat)

Another significant narrative was shared when the STs described their initial introductions in the EFL class. The STs introduced themselves and the learners then interviewed them, curiously asking all sorts of questions. The STs talked about their looks, but then, contrary to expectations, and much to the STs' surprise, one learner commented about the color of her own eyes, as follows:

> *Fragment 8*
> There were several interesting and memorable moments. In the first class, with the adult learners' group, Rachel asked us to introduce and describe ourselves. I then observed something that Rachel had already mentioned about the learners' social perceptions in relation to colors, even in congenital blindness: a blind student asked us about our eye color, adding after our responses that she thought green eyes were very pretty and she would really like to have green eyes. (Pat)

Hair also came up as a topic, and Amy's afro hairstyle was a big hit. She laughingly described the scene to us in class, for as soon as she realized that the learners had no idea what she was talking about as she described her hairstyle, she pointedly asked them to touch her hair and thus 'see' it. The learners loved this learning opportunity (and loved her hair). After these initial interactions, guided by Rachel, the ice broke, and the STs felt part of the classroom community.

Another teaching tool which immediately caught the STs' attention regards one of the five senses that teachers definitely do not usually resort to in class, touching. However, impelled by a need to interact with learners who cannot see, the cooperating teacher has developed a 'touch language': Rachel communicates with her learners using touch as a non-verbal strategy, as we can see below:

> *Fragment 9*
> In this class something which surprised me since the first class was the manner in which the teacher employs touch, touching the learner's arm ... (Pat)

> *Fragment 10*
> Another relevant point refers to the interaction strategies developed by the teacher through touching ... it's a two-way-street, impacting the student-teacher relationship. (Tina)

In their internship reports, a good deal is devoted to the issue of how Rachel is able to communicate just by touching. Different touches convey different meanings, and the STs realized that touching can potentially create yet another channel for classroom dialogue with blind learners. Although no eye contact and gestures are possible, Rachel's 'touch language' seems to encapsulate the visual tools that the teacher could otherwise use with sighted learners. The STs obviously knew they were not expected to learn Rachel's system, but they realized how touching becomes a meaningful tool in this context. There was another significant aspect that came up when the STs shared their field experience, for they soon realized the following on entering the ICPAC classroom:

> *Fragment 11*
> Strategies developed and used by the teacher during the class – a U-shaped seating arrangement ... (Pat)

This arrangement was the brainchild of a ST the previous year, when, after a couple of classes, he came up with the suggestion of a closer seating arrangement, U-shaped, in which the teacher can literally sit in the middle of the group, practically within arm's reach of all of the learners. Therefore, in addition to this proximity contributing to quicker non-verbal interaction (through touch), it also facilitated verbal interaction, crucial in a classroom where visual communication is impossible. This was a great contribution, a leadership opportunity for the ST, and Rachel immediately adopted the seating idea. For the four STs, 'the Circle' became a recurrent topic when sharing their practicum experiences in class.

Due to a sense of insecurity, at first the STs kept a distance and did not go near the circular seating arrangement. After some classes, they were gradually able to physically move towards the circle, and this movement, in turn, signaled an identity shift, as described below:

> *Fragment 12*
> Entering this semicircle was a challenge... as we gained ownership of the place – the physical space, as well as the place of professional identity – I perceived the potential of this configuration, not only encouraging learner interaction, but also aiding the development of our didactic strategies applied in the classes. (Tina)

The words above seem to crystallize the narrative surrounding 'the circle', which regularly emerged in the discussions at the university, creating a vague, non-verbalized metaphor, the circle as a physical seating arrangement and also as a symbolic social place, belonging to the professional teacher. Initially talking as teachers-to-be, there was a shift as they gained ownership of this place, and, as Fragment 12 reveals, the ST started speaking from a different social place, as a teacher.

Amy's weekly oral narratives from the field clearly addressed the tension regarding the circle and the teacher's chair. Distancing herself from the learners due to insecurity as an observer and, in her words, unable "to empower herself with the teacher's place", the discussions after each class revolved around overcoming this challenge. In this vein, the excerpt below indicates how she gradually gained ownership of her social place in the circle:

> *Fragment 13*
> One of my greatest challenges was going inside the circle, in the middle of the learners' [u-shaped] seats. Every day I wrote in my notebook that I had to enter the circle, and I gradually got closer. First I took a step forwards, towards the circle; then I stood near the tip, still outside the circle; when my teaching day got closer, I finally managed to go inside the circle. It was incredible, we have to celebrate each victory, even if it seems small. The cooperating teacher always gave us a lot of positive feedback regarding our victories, and never failed to call our attention whenever necessary. I entered the circle … (Amy)

For Amy, getting close to and entering the circle seemed like having to cross an ocean, no less. The poignant fragment above also signals a teacher identity shift, in dialogue with the verbal flux in the practicum, sustained by the co-supervision which emerged in this setting. Fragments 12 and 13 are also in dialogue with the following excerpt, which voices the insightful moment when Tina started to realize her new social place, thanks to a comment from a learner:

> *Fragment 14*
> In this context, minutes before our teaching started, I remembered the beginning of our experience here, and the episode when one of the learners called me teacher and she had to repeat this a few times till I understood that she was interacting with me. (Tina)

In hindsight, much to her amusement and perplexity, the ST realized that the learner had positioned her as a teacher – something that had not yet dawned on her. In this case, the ST's social identity was framed by how others saw her. It is learner-ST interaction which repositions Tina, the undergraduate/ student teacher, as a professional.

The internship phase is a pivotal moment in the undergraduate program. On the one hand, it is a period when some students opt out and, on the other hand, when student teachers decide to stay in the profession. The practicum can confirm what they had professionally planned in the first place and can also help hesitant STs overcome their professional doubts. Amy, Pat, and Tina, from the start, clearly wanted to become teachers. This was not the case with Vera, and the following excerpt reveals another emblematic student learning aspect in the practicum, related to a career choice:

> *Fragment 15*
> I sometimes thought about giving up, but I did not give in to discouragement. On analyzing the cooperating teacher's classes, I could notice that the manner in which she approached classroom contents was totally different from my past middle and high school teachers' approach. A practical and communicative way that always invited learners to participate in the learning process, they were not mere spectators in a class. When I had to teach (few opportunities, because of my insecurity), I did my best for my teaching practice to resemble the cooperating teacher's; however, due to fear, afraid of learners' questions and even of their improvised answers, I reversed to my past middle and high school teachers' approach. A centralizing teacher position bothers me, so I worked on removing this positioning in my practice.
>
> When we got to the last two classes, I had the feeling that I could have done so many things differently, in a better way; however, for me, learning has transformed the fear which existed in the beginning of the internship into a challenge to keep on in the profession.

The cooperating teacher's approach evokes school memories with past language teachers and conflicting issues arise, especially pertaining to insecurity and teacher-student interaction. Vera contrasts her teacher-centered school classes with the current student-centered approach, enhancing dialogue – in Freire's terms, respecting the freedom of the students. Amidst tensions, and with supportive co-supervision, Vera analyzes her actions and strengthens her identity as a teacher. In sum, the co-leadership experience in the practicum enhanced ST learning and change, as well as a sense of freedom among the teachers.

5 Reflections in Flux

What contributed to this successful co-leadership approach in the practicum? First of all, an important factor is that the cooperating teacher had precious time available for co-supervision, for this is a time-consuming process. Second, the cooperating teacher and university supervisor had an ongoing dialogue for years, developing mutual trust and understanding. Third, cohesive learning communities were established by both co-supervisors with the STs, in the field and at the university. Finally, the complex verbal flow that enveloped the cooperating teacher and university supervisor enabled co-supervision, 'making enough room' for the cooperating teacher to co-supervise and co-lead. It is relevant to add that this co-leader relationship is clearly a direct result of the cohesive group of university supervisors working together with the practicum in my department. Importantly, in line with Shulman (1988), as this chapter writing has yet again reminded me, "when we conduct educational research, we make the claim that there *is* method to our madness" (p. 16).

Dialogue and reflective writing are crucial in the educational process in the practicum. ST writing unveils the literacy events that Rachel developed in the practicum with creative learning tools, enhancing supervision. The selected fragments about the internship experience depict STs in transit between two institutions, ICPAC and university, and simultaneously in transit between student teacher and teacher identities, connected to academic and professional spheres. In sum, the fragments included here suggest teacher identity construction, unveiling student teacher literacy events in a practicum, whereby the cooperating teacher's actions signal co-supervision and co-leadership. Portraying life in the practicum, Pat's final words in her internship report offer some powerful insights.

> *Fragment 16*
> During this practicum, I was encouraged to challenge myself, to overcome limitations and to question pre-established conceptions. My definition of seeing nowadays is very different from the one I had before the internship, it has broadened. The internship had a crucial role, having me realize everything I am unable to see in the world, as Helen Keller pointed out in her text, *Three Days to See*. I finish this process happy and transformed by the beautiful and incisive reminder to see the world with other eyes, seeing in so many ways, and learning with each new point of view. (Pat)

In sum, on unveiling literacy events in a unique practicum experience, the fragments discussed in this chapter signal teacher identity construction and, in parallel, leadership development. The cooperating teacher's actions, in sync with my own since 2016 (when we first worked together in this inclusive internship context), have had an impact on several other undergraduate students over the years, besides the quartet discussed here, enhancing collaboration and teacher research.

Dedication

This chapter is dedicated to Antônio Eduardo de Oliveira Silva, student at the Instituto dos Cegos da Paraíba, whose reflective feedback and enthusiastic approach to life was so inspiring. Having just started university, unfortunately, he left us much too soon.

References

Amigues, R.(2004). Trabalho do professor e trabalho de ensino. Trabalho do professor e trabalho de ensino (Teacher's work and teaching work). In A. R. Machado (Ed.), *O ensino como trabalho: uma abordagem discursiva* [*Teaching as work: a discursive approach*] (pp. 35–53). EDUEL-FAPESP.

Bailey, F., Burkett, B., & Freeman, D. (2008). The mediating role of language in teaching and learning: A classroom perspective. In B. Spolsky & F. M. Hult (Eds.), *The handbook of educational linguistics* (pp. 606–625). Blackwell.

Bakhtin, M. (2000). *Estética da criação verbal* [*Aesthetics of verbal creation*] (3rd ed., M. E. Galvão, Trans.). Martins Fontes.

Barton, D., & Hamilton, M. (2000). Literacy practices. In D. Barton, M. Hamilton, & R. Ivanic (Eds.), *Situated literacies: Reading and writing in context* (pp. 7–15). Routledge.

Barton, D., Hamilton, M., & Ivanic, R. (Eds.). (2000). *Situated literacies: Reading and writing in context*. Routledge.

Benites, L. C., Sarti, F. M., & Souza Neto, S. (2015). De mestres de ensino fa formadores de campo no estágio supervisionado [From teaching masters to supervised internship field educators]. *Cadernos de Pesquisa, 45*(155), 110–117.

Brasil. (2002a, March 8). Conselho Nacional de Educação. Resolution #1. Proclaims the 'Diretrizes Curriculares Nacionais para a Formação de Professores da Educação Básica, em nível superior, curso de licenciatura, de graduação plena' [National curricular guidelines for teacher education in basic education, university level licensure]. In *Diário Oficial da União* [*Union Officia Daily paper*]. Brasília, Section 1, p. 8.

Brasil. (2002b, March 4). Conselho Nacional de Educação. Resolution #2. Proclaims the duration and time load duração of undergraduate licensing programs, school teacher education. In *Diário Oficial da União* [*Union Official Daily paper*]. Brasília, Section 1, p. 9.

Brasil. (2008, September 26). Law # 11788. Sets guidelines on student internships. In *Diário Oficial da União* [*Union Official Daily paper*]. Brasília, Section 1, pp. 3–4.

Brasil. (2015, July 1) Ministério da Educação, CNE. Resolution #2. *Curricular guidelines for university level initial and continued education for school teachers in basic education.*

Bronckart, J. P. (1999). *Atividade de linguagem, textos e discursos: Por um interacionismo sociodiscursivo* [*Language activity, texts and discourses: For sociodiscursive interactionism*]. EDUC.

Burton, J., Quirke, P., Reichmann, C., & Peyton, J. K. (2009). (Eds.). *Reflective writing: A way to lifelong teacher learning.* TESL-EJ, E-Book Edition. http://tesl-ej.org/books/reflective_writing.pdf

Clot, Y. (2007). *A função psicológica do trabalho* [*The psychological function of work*] (2nd ed., Adail Sobral, Trans. from French). Vozes. (Original work published 1999)

Freire, P. (1970). *Pedagogy of the oppressed.* Seabury Press.

Freire, P. (1996). *Letters to Cristina: Reflections on my life and work.* Routledge.

Keller, H. (1933). Three days to see. *The Atlantic Monthly, 151*(1), 35–42. https://www.theatlantic.com/past/docs/issues/33jan/keller.htm

Kleiman, A. B. (Ed.). (1995). *Os significados do letramento: uma nova perspectiva sobre as práticas sociais da escrita* [*The meanings of literacy: a new perspective on social practices and writing*]. Mercado de Letras.

Kleiman, A. B., & Reichmann, C. L. (2012). "Tive uma visão melhor da minha vida escolar": Letramentos híbridos e o relato fotobiográfico no estágio supervisionado ["I had a betterr perspective of my school life": Hybrid literacies and the reflective photobiography in the supervised internship]. *Caderno de Letras (UFPEL)* [*Letters notebook – Catholic University of Pelotas*], *18*, 156–175.

Machado, A. R. (Ed.). (2004). *O ensino como trabalho: Uma abordagem discursiva* [*Teaching as work: A discursive approach*]. EDUEL – FAPESP.

Medrado, B. P. (2012). Tornando-se professor: a compreensão de graduandos em Letras sobre a atividade educacional [Becoming a teacher: Undergraduates'comprehension of letters on an educational activity. In B. P. Medrado & C. L. Reichmann (Eds.), *Projetos e práticas na formação de professores de língua inglesa* [*Projects and practices in EFL teacher development*] (pp. 151–169). Editora da UFPB.

Medrado, B. P. (Ed.). (2014). *Deficiência visual e ensino de línguas estrangeiras: Políticas, formação e ações inclusivas* [*Visual deficiency and foreign language teaching: Politics, development and inclusive actions*]. Pontes Editora.

Medrado, B. P., & Dantas, R. (Eds.). (2019). *Materiais didáticos acessíveis de língua inglesa para alunos com deficiência visual* [*Accessible EFL didactic materials for blind learners*]. Ideia.

Okech, J. A. (2008). Reflective practice in group co-leadership. *The Journal for Specialists in Group Work, 33*(3), 236–252.

Portelance, L., Caron, J., & Martineau, S. (2016). Collaboration through knowledge sharing between cooperating teachers and university supervisors. *Brock Education Journal, 26*(1), 36–51.

Quirke, P. (2014). *Managing the language classroom.* Teachers of English to Speakers of Other Languages.

Reichmann, C. L. (2001). Teachers in dialogue: Exploring practice in an interactive professional journal. In J. Burton & M. Carroll (Eds.), *Journal writing* (pp. 125–135). Teachers of English to Speakers of Other Languages.

Reichmann, C. L. (2015). *Letras e letramentos: Escritaa situada, identidade ee trabalho docente no estágio supervisionado.* TRANS. Mercado de Letras.

Shulman, L. S. (1988). The disciplines of inquiry in education: An overview. In R. Jaeger (Ed.), *Complementary methods for research in education* (pp. 3–18). American Educational Teachers Association.

Souza Neto, S., Sarti, F. M., & Benites, L. C. (2011). Do ofício de aluno ao habitus profissional docente: desafios do estágio supervisionado [From learner apprenticeship to professional teacher habitus]. In *Anais do encontro de pesquisa em educação da região sudeste* [*Annals the Southeastern research in education meeting*] (pp. 1–11). UERJ-Unirio-UFRJ.

Street, B. (2003). What's "new" in new literacy studies? Critical approaches to literacy in theory and practice. *Current Issues in Comparative Education, 5*(2) 77–91.

Yalom, I. D., & Leszcz, M. (2005). *The theory and practice of group psychotherapy* (5th ed.). Basic Books.

CHAPTER 5

Visions and Realities: Doctoral Perspectives on Practice and Leadership

Jill Burton

John Dewey's impact on theorizing teaching has been profound. His works (e.g., 1910 and 1938) have led to many publications by educational researchers (e.g., Moon, 2004), as all of the chapters in this book attest. His influence on practice, while widespread, is harder to assess. Teaching approaches stimulated by reflection, such as inquiry-based teaching (e.g., Freeman, 1998) and action research (e.g., Burns, 1999), are enthusiastically received but difficult to incorporate into daily teaching practice without institutional support (Burton, 1997). Teachers sometimes adopt strategies such as journal writing and narratives (Burns & Burton, 2008; Burton & Carroll, 2001), which they find possible to organize for themselves and which give them some evidence of professional growth (Burton, 2009). However, teachers as students themselves may never have been shown how to use reflection as a learning tool, and it may not be until, as doctoral students on leadership pathways, that they are in a position to think deeply about teaching.

For many doctoral students with whom I have worked, these factors affect their understanding of doctoral study and approaches to leadership. In this chapter, I write as a doctoral supervisor and as a doctoral student about how writing might influence the interpretation of leadership in teaching. I began with two questions. Why do teachers of English as an additional language (EAL) become doctoral candidates? Where can reflective writing fit in doctoral students' practice of leadership?

I consider doctoral experiences of writing, my students' and my own, which emphasized reflective writing, and responses to a questionnaire (Burton, 2007) distributed to contributors to the *Case Studies of TESOL Practice* (Burton, series editor, 2001–2006). In both settings, many students and published writers were nominally in senior positions. Few would have described themselves as leaders. Rather, they saw themselves as middle managers, cogs in vertical chains of responsibility in which they were held responsible by those below and accountable to those above. This is not what being a leader means. Could a leadership perspective, one based on independence of outlook and responsible thinking, be encouraged in the doctoral community to which I belonged?

1 The Doctoral Environment

The Australian university where I was teaching had two main doctoral programs in education. One, for students who had completed master degrees with research and minor-thesis components, resulted in a Doctor of Philosophy (Ph.D.). The other, a Doctor of Education (D.Ed.), combined coursework in research methods with three research projects and a meta-analysis. In practice, both programs drew on the strengths of the other: Ph.D. students in education benefited from clearly structured D.Ed. research procedures, and D.Ed. students integrated three discrete research projects into a sequential program of professional learning.

Both programs highlighted the importance of students writing for private and public consumption throughout doctoral study, not just in the 'final' thesis or the project reports and meta-analysis. All students regularly submitted research diaries and reports to supervisors. They were also required to circulate, in draft form, research proposals, ethics protocols, study reports and data analyses, and chapters, for wider feedback from within the Teachers of English to Speakers of Other Languages (TESOL) research and practice community.

Due to these practices and some commonalities in students' research interests, supervisors inaugurated regular meetings, a teachers' research group (TRG), in which students could share research experiences and rehearse leading discussions on research processes, in particular, how to write for an academic readership (Burton, 2013). The meetings also widened students' exposure to writing and research beyond the TRG. For example, they discussed readings, and there were visiting speakers from time to time.

Students' teaching backgrounds, and my own background as a student and supervisor, added other dimensions to the discussions. These are considered below.

1.1 *The Students*

TRG students came mainly from Southeast Asia, a third from Thailand, and a third like me, resident in Australia (see Table 5.1). The students enrolled in the D.Ed. program either had no formal training as researchers or chose to focus on professional rather than academic goals. Apart from a couple of students, they taught EAL to tertiary students or were teacher educators in that sector (see Table 5.2). Many were on full-time scholarships. The rest were self-funded, part-time students. The majority sought career advancement. Students' research foci and methodologies fell into recognizable areas and patterns (see Tables 5.3 & 5.4).

Data collection usually involved the equivalent of a semester of field work, for which overseas students usually went back home. Their studies raised

TABLE 5.1   Cultural and educational backgrounds of students

Number	Country & main language	Sex F	Sex M	Education
7	Australia			
6	Thailand			
3	Vietnam	15	7	Masters
2	South Korea			
2	People's Republic of China (PRC)			
1	Indonesia			
1	The Philippines			

TABLE 5.2   Professional experience and goals

Number	Professional experience	Number	Funding	Number	Goals
8	Tertiary instructors	12	Full-time scholarships	7	Senior academic, teacher
6	Institute of technology lecturers			7	University lecturer
6	University lecturers: English & teacher education	10	Part-time, mainly self-supporting	5	Program administrator
1	National curriculum consultant			3	Specialist, self-enrichment
1	School teacher				

different ethical considerations from those of the Australian-based students. Research participants in Asian countries had few rights compared with those of their research-hosting institutions, research plans not infrequently needed

TABLE 5.3   Research foci

Curriculum & course design	Needs analysis, materials design, teaching methodologies
Language	Learning, interlanguage, grammars, discourse analysis, Englishes, cross-cultural practices
Teacher education	Practicum, reflective practice, action research
Learning	Plagiarism, independent learning, reflective practice
Tertiary learners	Reflective writing, academic writing

TABLE 5.4   Research methodologies

Component 1	Component 2	Component 3	Meta-analysis/Discussion
Literature review	*Data collection & pilot studies*	*Data analysis*	– *DEd students* analysed the impact of Stages 1, 2 & 3
	Questionnaires	Data reporting & analysis	
	Interviews		
	Case study		
Variety of combinations and weightings between stages/ projects			– *PhD students* wrote evaluations & discussion chapters

renegotiation once data collection was underway on site, and scholarship conditions could conflict with students' research goals. Supervisors maintained student support during the field-data-collection period via E-journals and, later, Skype; they also made site visits.

Doctoral years can prove to be a period of continual readjustment, which raised questions for students and for supervisors. In circumstances that students cannot wholly control, how can they frame studies to meet funding goals and satisfy their own beliefs? To what extent was it legitimate to pursue personal goals rather than institutional goals? When might scholarship providers be persuaded to accept different directions? And, how can such questions be addressed as part of the doctoral process?

Many overseas students were middle-aged with families, who made considerable sacrifices to enable their studies abroad. Sometimes, one parent came to Australia to study and then the other, with the children staying home with one parent at a time. These families might become one-parent families for eight years or longer. Alternatively, children stayed home with grandparents while both parents studied in Australia simultaneously, missing out on vital years of their children's growth. Other students brought children with them, enrolling them in local schools to learn English in the Australian education system, with partners visiting on limited-period, temporary work visas. Doctoral study had to be practical and accommodate family considerations.

1.2 *My Background as Supervisor and Fellow Student*

I joined the university sector at a time when a master degree, combined with international research publications and academic publishing experience, automatically put me on the university's research register. However, the demand for doctoral qualifications in senior TESOL positions began to intensify worldwide and, while I could see the struggles that students faced, their joy when successful was delightful to witness. To adopt a line from a popular film, I wanted what they were having, so I enrolled as a doctoral student at the university where I was already a doctoral supervisor. I went through doctoral study at the same time as some of my students, and my supervisor was someone my students knew.

The doctoral program in which I was enrolled was different from the Ph.D. and D.Ed. programs, however. It was a doctoral degree by portfolio of research publications, accompanied by an exegesis. I submitted ten journal articles and book chapters published over the previous decade. Selection afforded multiple opportunities for reflection, which came to underpin my research methodology. Choosing publications revealed salient threads in my work. I noticed what interests and expertise I had built on along the way. It was more of a staged career than the scatter-gun one I had suspected. Compelled to reflect on this work-life for a doctorate, a clearer understanding emerged of how teacher learning actually evolves.

I found that the selected publications featured reflecting and writing, although these features were not named as such in the earlier writings. While I was now itching to edit pieces I'd written earlier in the hindsight of what I was discovering from re-reading them, the following forward-looking aims prevailed:

- to examine how teacher knowledge can be constructed and written by teachers for other teachers in ways that do not separate them from the classroom and also help them to develop as leaders in their professional contexts;
- to demonstrate through a reflective exegesis how professional understanding develops in writing over a ten-year period;
- to write a substantial exegesis, equivalent to the theses and meta-analyses-plus-projects my students were constructing in Ph.D. or D.Ed. programs.

I had more freedom than my students in situating my doctoral study in my work and in how I wrote, but my situation raised one different challenge. Whereas my students were striving to move beyond the university and join the wider academic community, I strove to stay in it and advance further. Many career moves in the university sector were becoming increasingly impossible, because I didn't have a doctorate. Without a doctorate, I could now quickly be ruled out in the first round in any application process. But this didn't leave me professionally isolated, unlike many TRG students. I still had other, significant support groups, such as my co-writers in this book. In the following sections, I critique doctoral writing and reflection and the extent to which they affected and influenced my students and myself.

2 Doctoral Methodologies

The methodology I adopted is summarized in Table 5.5.

TABLE 5.5 Reflective writing methodology

Stage	Data
1	1. Curriculum vitae
	2. Career narrative
2	10 core narratives
3	Core narratives categorized as points of departure for Chapters 2, 3, & 4
4	Chapters 2, 3, & 4 drafts, including
	1. additional internal narratives
	2. end-of-chapter reflections
5	Chapter 5, final reflections
6	Chapter 1, incorporating Stage 1 data, research rationale, and methodology

Note: Literature review incorporated in all chapters as another layer of reflective writing.

2.1 *Writing and Reading between the Lines*

I began by writing a CV and a career narrative and subjecting them to contrastive analysis. While narrative highlighted my lived experience, the CV, written to convince rather than to raise questions, lacked the nuance of the narrative, which questioned, probed, and explained. The two texts were included in the first of five exegesis chapters. It was the last chapter to be written. My thinking and writing interacted continually throughout the study, generating a recursive, narrative procedure.

2.2 *Reflective Narrative*

After writing the career-focused texts, I wrote a reflective narrative on each of the publications comprising the research portfolio in my thesis, ten core narratives in all. Four introduced Chapter 2, and three each preceded Chapters 3 and 4. The chapters contained other reflective narratives and end-of-chapter reflections, bridging the thinking between chapters and demonstrating development in the thinking. Chapter 5 was a meta-analysis of the preceding chapters and ended with postdoctoral points of departure. Then Chapter 1 was written, foregrounding the study, its starting points, rationale, and methodology.

I found narrative writing to be a creative research instrument. As Bakhtin (1991), Clandinen and Connelly (2000), Elbaz-Luwisch (2005), Ricoeur (1991), and Riessman (1993) can be shown to collectively argue, narrative encourages dialogue, interpretation, and constructive doubt. Its intention is to communicate through addressing familiar questions, such as 'What?', 'Who?', 'How?', 'Why?', 'What does it all mean?' These questions are central to the reflective writing methodology that the five writers in this book have already described (Burton et al., 2009), and are fundamental questions for teachers.

Narrative as research methodology afforded me perspective (Richardson, 1990) and stance (Ely et al., 1997); that is, triangulation. Reflection added another dimension. Instead of disrupting, narratives and reflections offered alternative meanings, what Richardson (1997) calls 'pleated' text.

In sum, my methodology was intended to

1. make my research stance and thinking steps open;
2. demonstrate how I used reflection in my own practice;
3. demonstrate learning as lifelong inquiry;
4. foreground questions rather than answers;
5. be constructively provocative.

All university research is structured around research proposals and ethics protocols formalized through a hierarchy of committees. Proposals and protocols focus on planning frameworks and procedures but, as the distinction above between curriculum vitae and career narratives suggests, frameworks and procedures are bones not the flesh – the writing – of research. While my students were unable to take the liberties I was taking, in our one-to-one meetings we regularly discussed the extent to which they were having to reshape plans and expectations as they worked. Any hopes of security in a steady, progressive path from Chapter 1 (Introduction), through Chapter 2 (Literature Review), Chapter 3 (Research Methodology), and so on, rapidly evaporated.

Research processes not only require renegotiation from time to time, they prompt new reading.

2.3 Reviewing Literature

Literature review is central in all research processes. My doctoral students expected, as was customary, to present discrete literature review chapters. In the D.Ed. program, for example, it might form one of the three research projects or be incorporated as sections in each of the three projects. As a supervisor in this program and the Ph.D. program, I encouraged students also to refer to literature in other chapters, wherever it seemed relevant, to adopt an organic approach to reading, thinking, and writing.

In my own doctoral research, reviewing literature became an explicit source of reflection, functioning as another source of triangulation. Chapters 2, 3, and 4 focused, respectively, on
- *Learning TESOL*, i.e., theorizing practice;
- *Practicing TESOL*, i.e., curriculum;
- *Writing TESOL*, i.e., reflection and publication.

These chapters also surveyed specific commercial and university press publications for teachers and critiqued publications for teachers issued by the international TESOL organization in the United States.

The TESOL publications examined were series of reflective case studies and narratives on teaching. As I had been connected with the TESOL organization throughout my career, they provided a relevant frame for reflection. Although the International Association for Teachers of English as a Foreign Language (IATEFL) based in the U.K. suggested an alternative perspective, its publishing function was less developed, and my professional connections with it were not as close. Also, the two countries approached teacher education somewhat differently. Although generalizations are always questionable, I found that, in North America, teachers were more likely to be encouraged to enroll in doctoral programs as a way to make progress in their careers. In the U.K., Australia, and New Zealand, these professional career pathways have developed more recently.

While for me as a doctoral student, literature opened up connections with teachers and researchers, few other TRG students thought of it as part of their world, if only because reading material was hard to access where they taught. Unease with it manifested early in students' writing, with many students failing to see historical connections in the literature. They might cite twenty-first-century researchers as influences on twentieth-century research, a chronological impossibility, for example. So, how to use research literature was a common topic of TRG conversations.

Engaging with literature is a striking example of the fact that however tidy and orderly research can appear to readers, writing about it can be confusing. This need be no cause for alarm, according to Annie Dillard, who believes that writing, if you let it, can take you 'in a twinkling, from an expression of your notions to an epistemological tool' (1990, p. 3). Texts that discourage argument are 'shut texts' (Duncker, 1996, p. 112). My students favored this kind of writing, not only having found many examples of it in the academic literature they were reading but also not wanting to have their research questioned. But such writing didn't interest me. Writers who invite debate own – take responsibility for – what they write. However, I couldn't expect my students to follow me down that path to leadership. They had different expectations and priorities.

2.4   Writing as Possibility

Reflective writing has helped me realize what being a leader as a teacher could mean. My portfolio and exegesis aimed to demonstrate my understanding of ways that it can open several pathways for its readers, through
- *publications*, which suggest a chronology of inquiry;
- *chapters and narratives*, which highlight dominant themes;
- *a writing methodology*, which demonstrates the interrelationship of practice, reflection, and learning.

My writing was 'more argumentative' than that of my students. Whatever satisfaction my students learned to find in writing for themselves about their research diminished at the thought of writing for others. This is not unusual, as I had earlier found as evaluator of the Languages In-Service Project for Teachers (LIPT) of languages other than English (1997). At that time, I also discovered Elbow's work (1973, 1994), in which he reported his fear of writing, which didn't disappear until he wrote as himself rather than as a student or teacher. When the connection between writing in educational settings and evaluation is remembered, Elbow's revelation is not unexpected, and doctoral programs, like other formal education programs, rely on writing to communicate and to assess learning.

Following Kamler and Thomson's recommendations (2006), and because of students' general fear of writing, TRG supervisors emphasized writing as a practice throughout doctoral study.

While Kamler and Thomson were setting forth an expanded role for writing in scholarly practice, Garman and Piantanida (2006) discovered, rather like Elbow, that writing raised questions of authenticity for writers. They encouraged a group of completing doctoral candidates to reflect on how they had rendered researching and writing more transparent in their theses. For some, this had meant treating the thesis as an essay, or as a narrative. For others, the thesis itself became the heuristic inquiry. These methodologies freed them to speculate and imagine, to engage with, their future roles in the profession – scholarly experiences I respected.

Through my doctoral study, I wanted to *experience* learning and to display that experience. For me, that meant putting reading and writing at the heart of practice, but could I ask such engagement of my students?

3   Reflections

Different learning preferences and goals gave all TRG participants – students and supervisors – pause for thought. Clearly, circumstance is an additional factor in professional practice and careers, to which pre- and in-service provisions can only ever partly respond. TRG supervisors returned, time and time again, to consideration of students' personal professional goals. It turned out that some students, despite being mid- or late-career doctoral candidates, were not fully reconciled to the teaching careers they found themselves immersed in. For the rest, a doctorate in teaching represented the pinnacle of development on the path to endorsement as a leader.

It was evident from what TRG students told me in my 2013 study, though, that doctoral study was for all of them a first, serious opportunity to pause, examine, and expand their expertise. It is not inappropriate to call this time something of a luxury, despite the inevitable stress that studying of a different kind in an unfamiliar environment imposes. For non-Australian students, one challenge was performing in class. Initially intimidated, these students came to welcome chances to contest and question aloud. They also pondered the implications of this sort of student behavior for their own teaching. What if they encouraged students to discuss and debate in their own classes? How could it be managed within the constraints of teacher-directed learning and large classes? Was this a practical teaching approach? Could it be piloted in their doctoral projects? Overall, they realized that the strengths of the university doctoral program were the reflecting, mentoring, sharing, and development of community that these activities fostered. Labels like 'student' and 'teacher' could be shrugged off, at least for some of the time, and written reflection proved to be one of the spurs.

3.1   *Writing as Community*

The community that the TRG became can be characterized as a learning culture (Bruner, 1996) of distributed expertise (Shulman, 2004), a community of practice (Wenger, 1998) that collaboratively theorized, sharing data and documentation – epitomizing Wenger's concept of reification. Reflecting and writing pushed thinking deep. Discussions moved from factual inquiry ('What's happening here?' 'How did it happen?') to interpretations ('Why did it happen?' 'What exactly does this mean for my study, and for my future teaching?'), which supported even deeper reflections.

Though encircled by the requirements of an award-bearing program, as a community of practice, the TRG was successful. Participants forged bonds that gave them lasting professional and personal connections.

In this safe communal setting, leadership could be rehearsed. Supervisors discovered that many of the doctoral students were seen as leaders in their work settings. Student demeanor tended to obscure this, due to the doctoral setting and, in some cases, to perceptions of learning as a passive behavior. As a supervisor, I countered this by describing leadership as taking responsibility, first of all, for one's own learning and practice. Under this definition, all TRG students could call themselves leaders, regardless of their work title. It wasn't a question of being a 'program manager', 'faculty dean', or 'curriculum specialist'. Being a 'classroom teacher' was title enough.

Effective teacher-leaders are effective observers, which is where reflection comes in. Implementing curriculum means documenting, reflecting, learning, and building on practice. This is teaching as leadership. There is no need to step outside the classroom to experience leadership (though a title and higher salary are generally the reward for those who do, an unfortunate observation on how teaching is perceived as a profession). The two doctoral programs in which I was a supervisor aimed to support teachers to 'think leadership', to see a doctorate as a stepping stone into lifelong professional learning and leadership, whether their work settings were classrooms, offices, or board rooms. In each setting, teachers, like other professionals, are responsible for their actions and futures. How can teachers lead others if they can't lead themselves?

In the TRG, however, teachers as students were no longer fronting classrooms as experts in their own settings. They were seeking new skills and knowledge. While doctoral supervisors promoted reflective writing within the TRG as a way to support them in taking charge of their learning, almost without exception, the prospect of writing for the wider academic community alarmed them.

3.2   *Academic Practices*

Teachers are generally assumed to be successful writers (Ganobcsik-Williams, 2004, 2006). Bad experiences as school learners, however, have imbued many of them with a reluctance to write for others. As Casanave (2002, p. 176) and other researchers (e.g., Ivanic, 1998; Margolis & Romero, 1998) point out, there is more at stake for doctoral students as writers than adopting a style and genre. Academic writing has its own social practices. For whom you are writing is as important as who is writing and what is written – a cardinal reason for Casanave and Vandrick (2003), Kamler and Thomson (2006), and Richardson (1997), among others, to stress the learning potential for students in writing throughout doctoral study.

Beyond this, those teachers who as doctoral candidates conquer fear of writing for others can shape how teaching is represented outside the classroom. Choosing authentic writing forms that both represent teaching knowledge and meet doctoral and academic expectations, however, is challenging to address simultaneously in doctoral programs, and is rarely attempted.

Laurel Richardson portrays how she addressed her own concerns about writing as a doctoral candidate. Her thesis (published as a book, 1997) consists of papers with braided themes written over a ten-year period of teaching. She created a 'pleated' text, interweaving papers with 'writing-stories' as forewords and afterwords (p. 1). A leading example of what reflection and narrative can achieve, the book subverts a conventional thesis chronology, remaining true to her focus on how to represent herself as a teacher. In support of how she wrote, she argued that writing always tells the writer's story, whether the writer intends that or not, so writers should own their stories rather than write ones they think readers want.

Phan Le Ha (2008) is another writer who openly addressed the dilemma of representation in her writing. She chose to write personally, her critique demonstrating how, as a Vietnamese academic writer researching English as an international language (EIL), she managed to maintain her cultural identity. She concluded that representation in writing is about writers' continuity as individuals, about who they are, who they were, and who they are becoming (p. 193). Linda Cooper (2014), writing about the dissertation experiences of masters students in a South African university, found that years of accumulated teaching knowledge can be discarded when formal writing registers are adopted, but 'if students grasp how to exercise their agency strategically ... they may find ways not only to express their own experiential knowledge' (p. 45) but also to attain some professional influence.

TRG doctoral students found leading-through-writing, as Le Ha and Richardson chose and Cooper advocates, perilous to contemplate. Could their own writing stories interest examiners, let alone be considered important to other readers? Traditionally, examiners have awarded doctorates based mainly or solely on theses, and journal editors and publishers assess submissions for publication via blind reviews. Thus, writing is a vital skill that creates and binds academic and professional communities.

How then to proceed? Kamler and Thomson's solution (2006) relies on three axioms:
1. Writing well has to be practiced and learned.
2. Writing is construction as much as representation.
3. Thesis composition involves constructing a life as a teacher-learner and researcher as much as it concerns demonstrating knowledge.

Doctoral supervisors such as Ely et al. (1997) emphasize writing's importance in learning processes, while Swales (1990, 2004) highlights its discursive potential, as do Winter and Badley (2007). On the grounds that learning is always provisional, the latter promote doctoral writing as continuing conversations between writer and readers. They question, therefore, why students as writers would pretend to have academic authority that they don't yet have. Casanave (2002) notes that open, honest writing is capable of rigor and that it can make ideas happen.

Rather than expand student initiative, however, contributors to Ravelli and Ellis (2004) and Zamel and Spack (1998) favored strategies that increase structured supervision, such as more practice-based graduate assignments and feedback on classroom practice. Nonetheless, there are interesting differences of opinion in Zamel and Spack's volume. Lu's advice (pp. 71–83) is to be a silent writer, that is, to damp down debate, whereas Spellmeyer (1998) points out the dishonesty of pretending that writing has no writer behind it (pp. 105–122). So much academic writing is silent, and novice writers mimic those writers whom they regard as successful, protests Blanton (1998, pp. 219–236), mimicry that deliberately masks meaning and ownership of ideas (see also, Hyland, 1998, on hedging, which has similar effects). Delpit (1998, pp. 207–218) recommends compromise: Structure doctoral study so that students become bi-discoursal writers, learning to write separately for teaching and for academic audiences.

That published writing, in addition to a thesis, is increasingly a requirement of doctoral study and that teachers increasingly see a doctorate as a leadership pathway offer some hope that teachers will eventually develop more powerful written voices. However, in recent years, the emphasis in universities and society on vocational education and client satisfaction (Lee & Danby, 2012) makes it harder still for teachers as doctoral writers to write imaginatively as potential teacher-leaders rather than as the academics or managers, which they see as their only career futures. Broadening the range of acceptable writing styles in doctoral programs so that it is more inclusive of teaching discourse and values, therefore, is one way for the profession to progress as well as to promote teachers as its leaders.

3.3 *Practicing Academe, Writing Practice*

Included in my doctoral research is a survey I conducted (in 2007) of writing experiences of authors in a 21-volume case studies series, of which I was series editor between 2001 and 2006. The series was expected to encourage teacher contributions. As Stoynoff commented in his review of the Series (2004), school teachers (as opposed to tertiary teachers) are underrepresented among its authors. Most respondents described themselves primarily as academics who also taught and were administrators.

Respondents published research articles and teaching materials. The overall perception was that publication was essential to advance their careers. But since writing had to be fitted around office hours and teaching, it was frequently stressful. Collaborative writing, although productive, was difficult to organize, so it was rarely engaged in. Two-thirds of the respondents never sought feedback on what they wrote, other than unavoidable reviews from journal editors and publishers. Some of these published writers reported feeling professionally insecure and uncertain about how publishing processes really operate. I was surprised to find that these respondents, as published authors, had not overcome the sorts of unease expressed by TRG students. For both sets of writers, academe was evidently a gated community.

Asked to describe their experiences of reflective writing in the survey, those writers who did use it were enthusiastic:

> There's nothing I dislike about it ... Sorry if that sounds like Pollyanna. (#25–27)

> It has become part of what I do and perhaps who I am. (#3)

> I enjoy writing as an activity; it's mentally stimulating, and it puts me in touch with others even though I work at home. (#4)

> It helps me make sense of my life. (#5)

> It's a means of thinking for me. Writing freely, whether it's jotting down ideas on the spur of the moment or sitting down deliberately to think and work through ideas, helps the ideas come. And beyond that, once the ideas get down on paper, writing about them helps me clarify them in my mind. (#6)

Such comments confirm that personal, reflective writing has, at least for some teacher-academics, become a learning tool.

Elsewhere, Miller (2008) writes of the struggle for teachers in turning themselves into writers and the dilemma that she and others faced in combining teaching with academe. She employs conversations with another teacher and with herself as academic, reader, and practitioner, and imaginary ones with herself as a different teacher. It is powerful, rigorous writing, which successfully takes readers on a vicarious exploration of her thinking and practice. Peeler's chapter in the same collection (Burns & Burton, 2008) candidly reports grappling with combining doctoral study and classroom teaching, and switching to academic teaching. Miller and Peeler demonstrate that writing can problematize without pretending order when there is none – open writing that is as rigorous and delicate as it is powerful and truthful.

So, while these writers describe their difficulties as teachers writing, they also exemplify how it can be done.

TRG processes encouraged students to reflect on their composing experiences. Most common were expressions of dismay at completing a draft thesis chapter only to find its conclusion contradicting its starting point. As a supervisor, I probed the writing processes that had produced the draft. What had they set out to write? How had they gone about it? Why did they think the draft under discussion had turned out the way it had? Students' strongest reaction was always, "'I must 'make' the beginning fit the conclusion'", also that that would be easiest. They hesitated to recognize that what a conclusion offered them was a constructive starting point for a second draft and that they might reach a 'new' conclusion. Discussions might proceed along these lines: "But I won't have a conclusion anymore if I use it to introduce the new draft". "Yes, you will". "How is that possible?" "If you use it as your new starting point, and let it, it can take you there, it can 'write' you there".

More ready myself as a doctoral student to contemplate 'false' ends as new beginnings, to work with and through writing, as Annie Dillard (1990) recommends, I used this kind of 'work' as a scaffold for my doctoral writing and included it as 'data-work' in the narratives and reflections I wrote for my exegesis.

Rereading the earliest publications I intended to include in my doctoral portfolio as I began to study, I realized that I used to aim for an academic voice of guarded authority. My lack of actual authority – and by extension, my lack of authenticity as a writer – embarrassed me now. The writing wasn't convincing. Who was I writing for? Could it possibly have been useful? Why do teachers who want professional advancement continue trying to write this way? It is because they feel that though they wouldn't choose to, this is what is required of them.

Although such professional dilemmas remain, researchers are gradually becoming more interested in writing as a doctoral research methodology (e.g., Golden-Biddle & Lock, 1997; Holliday, 2002; Richardson, 2003; and, as already mentioned, Kamler & Thomson, 2006), which encourages more adventurous (still disciplined) writing. Thus, there is some visible progress in the literature, though many more teachers are needed as writers who become part of the literature on teacher learning and knowledge building. I like to think now that, through writing reflectively, inquiry can genuinely fire teachers' lives and practice. Everything I write now comes from that perspective. Is it what other teachers want for themselves? If not, why not? Should those in leading positions in the profession encourage it?

4 Proflections

Professional renewal is almost always a struggle for practicing teachers. Long ago, Schön commented:

> On the high ground, manageable problems lend themselves to solutions through the application of research-based theory and technique. In the swampy lowland, messy, confusing problems defy technical solution. The irony of this situation is that the problems of the high ground tend to be relatively unimportant to individuals or society at large, however great their technical interest may be, while in the swamp lie the problems of greatest human concern. (1987, p. 1)

His comment shows not only the divide between teaching practice and deciding what's important in teaching but also the lack of communication between teachers and managers. One reason for this is how leadership is defined. I argue, in response to Schön, that if the people on the low ground dared to look upwards, they might find ways to climb and reach the high ground. In Chapter 3 of my doctoral thesis, I pointed out that 'teaching' is much more than 'implementing'. It is 'planning, implementing, and reflecting'. It is much more than 'compliance' with curriculum; it is *engagement* and, to become leaders, teachers have to engage with what learning means – and communicate that engagement.

Doctoral study provides teachers probably the longest opportunity they will ever have to engage with practice, but few teacher education programs truly acknowledge the relevance of teachers' own experiences as school-learners in that engagement process. Jackson's (1986) and Lortie's (2002) research studies on this are still relevant. Leading as a teacher means learning and demonstrating to students how to learn. TRG members whom I interviewed (2013) told me how good and bad teachers they had had when at school influenced the learners and teachers they became. The classroom is a powerful social force. Leaders, I believe, are learners who take responsibility for what they learn and teach, look to the future, and guide the less expert. Leadership that begins in the classroom can go well beyond it.

Leadership challenges for teachers include the following:
1. How to remain true to beliefs; i.e., act authentically;
2. How to ask good questions;
3. How to identify and respond to learning needs in the classroom;
4. How to be responsible for learning in the classroom.

Meanwhile, doctoral programs are often where teachers seeking leadership education turn. Many graduates of such programs who have gone on to leadership positions are reluctant to talk about the challenges they met on the way. They are also disinclined to encourage others to approach their own careers differently, by writing frankly from their own experience about learning and teaching.

But this, I think, is what teachers as doctoral students and teachers who see themselves as potential leaders should be encouraged to do. It is how published writers Laurel Richardson, Phan Le Ha, Jennifer Miller, and Eleanor Peeler, cited in this chapter, have written – honestly, vividly, and rigorously. Progressive reflection underpins their writing. These writers tell their own stories, but they do more. They offer exemplars that other teachers can learn from. It is how teachers can lead the profession and how all of us can communicate and learn.

Dedication

This chapter is dedicated to Dr. Ngoc Ba Doan, a TRG doctoral student and graduate, who became a valued colleague and friend. Sadly, he died recently, much too young, having achieved much but with more he wanted to do for the profession. He is much missed.

References

Bakhtin, M. M. (1991). *The dialogic imagination: Four essays by M. M. Bakhtin* (M. Holquist, Ed.). University of Texas Press.
Blanton, L. L. (1998). Discourse, artifacts, and the Ozarks: Understanding academic literacy. In V. Zamel & R. Spack (Eds.), *Negotiating academic literacies: Teaching and learning across languages and cultures* (pp. 219–236). Lawrence Erlbaum.
Bruner, J. (1996). *The culture of education.* Harvard University Press.

Burns, A. (1999). *Collaborative action research for English language teachers*. Cambridge University Press.

Burns, A., & Burton, J. (Eds.). (2008). *Language teacher research in Australia and New Zealand*. Teachers of English to Speakers of Other Languages.

Burton, J. (1997). Sustaining language teachers As researchers of their own practice. *Canadian Modern Language Review/La Revue Canadienne des Langues Vivantes, 54*(11), 84–109.

Burton, J. (2008). Use of writing in teacher reflection [Questionnaire distributed to *Case studies in TESOL practice* contributors]. In *Writing TESOL: Constructing teaching in a TESOL world* (Appendix 4.1) [PhD thesis, University of South Australia, Adelaide].

Burton, J. (2009). Reflective writing – Getting to the heart of teaching and learning. In J. Burton, J. K. Peyton, P. Quirke, & C. Reichmann (Eds.), *Reflective writing as lifelong learning in language education* (pp. 1–11). TESL-EJ, E-Book Edition. http://tesl-ej.org/books/reflective_writing.pdf.

Burton, J. (2013). An informal community of language teachers. In C. L. Reichmann (Ed.), *Diàrios Reflexivos de Professores de Linguas: Ensinar, Escrever, Refazer (-Se)* [*Teaching, writing, and self-making: Teacher journals and literacies*] (pp. 285–300). Pontes Editores.

Burton, J., & Carroll, M. (Eds.). (2001). *Journal writing*. Teachers of English to Speakers of Other Languages.

Burton, J. (Series Ed.). (2001–2006). *Case studies in TESOL practice* (21 Vols.). Teachers of English to Speakers of Other Languages.

Burton, J., Peyton, J. K., Quirke, P., & Reichmann, C. (Eds.). (2009). *Reflective writing as lifelong learning in language education*. TESL-EJ, E-Book Edition. http://tesl-ej.org/books/reflective_writing.pdf

Casanave, C. P. (2002). *Writing games: Multicultural case studies of academic literacy practices in higher education*. Lawrence Erlbaum.

Casanave, C. P., & Vandrick, S. (Eds.). (2003). *Writing for scholarly publication: Behind the scenes in language education*. Lawrence Erlbaum.

Clandinin, D. J., & Connelly, F. M. (2000). *Narrative inquiry: Experience and story in qualitative research*. Jossey-Bass.

Cooper, L. (2014). "Does my experience count?" The role of experiential knowledge in the research writing of postgraduate adult learners. In L. Thesen & L. Cooper (Eds.), *Risk in academic writing: Postgraduate students, their teachers and the making of knowledge* (pp. 27–47). Multilingual Matters.

Delpit, L. D. (1998). The politics of teaching literate discourse. In V. Zamel & R. Spack (Eds.), *Negotiating academic literacies: Teaching and learning across languages and cultures* (pp. 207–218). Lawrence Erlbaum.

Dewey, J. (1938). *Experience and education*. Simon & Schuster/Free Press Imprint.

Dewey, J. (2012). *How we think*. Martino Publishing. (Original work published 1910)
Dillard, A. (1990). *The writing life*. Harper Perennial.
Duncker, P. (1996). *Hallucinating Foucault*. Bloomsbury Publishing.
Elbaz-Luwisch, F. (2005). *Teachers' voices: Storytelling and possibility*. Information Age Publishing.
Elbow, P. (1973). *Writing without teachers*. Oxford University Press.
Elbow, P. (1994). *Writing for learning – Not just for demonstrating learning*. University of Massachusetts.
Ely, M., Vinz, R., Downing, M., & Anzul, M. (Eds.). (1997). *On writing qualitative research: Living by words*. Falmer Press.
Freeman, D. (1998). *Doing teacher-research: From inquiry to understanding*. Heinle & Heinle.
Ganobcsik-Williams, L. (2004). *A report on the teaching of academic writing in UK higher education*. Royal Literary Fund.
Ganobcsik-Williams, L. (Ed.). (2006). *Teaching academic writing in UK higher education: Theories, practices, and models*. Palgrave Macmillan.
Garman, N., & Piantanida, M. (Eds.). (2006). *The authority to imagine: The struggle towards representation in dissertation writing*. Peter Lang.
Golden-Biddle, K., & Locke, K. D. (1997). *Composing qualitative research*. Sage Publications.
Holliday, A. (2002). *Doing and writing qualitative research*. Sage Publications.
Hyland, K. (1998). *Hedging in scientific research articles*. John Benjamins.
Ivanic, R. (1998). *Writing and identity: The discoursal construction of identity in academic writing*. John Benjamins.
Jackson, P. (1986). *The practice of teaching*. Teachers College Press.
Kamler, B., & Thomson, P. (2006). *Helping doctoral students write: Pedagogies for supervision*. Routledge.
Lee, A., & Danby, S. (Eds.). (2012). *Reshaping doctoral education: International approaches and pedagogies*. Routledge.
Le Ha, P. (2008). *Teaching English as an international language: Identity, resistance and negotiation*. Multilingual Matters.
Lortie, D. C. (2002). *Schoolteacher: A sociological study* (2nd ed.). University of Chicago Press. (Original work published 1975)
Lu, M.-Z. (1998). From silence to words: Writing as struggle. In V. Zamel & R. Spack (Eds.), *Negotiating academic literacies: Teaching and learning across languages and cultures* (pp. 71–83). Lawrence Erlbaum.
Margolis, E., & Romero, T. (1998). "The department is very male, very white, very old, and very conservative": The functioning of the hidden curriculum in graduate sociology departments. *Harvard Educational Review, 68*(1), 1–32.

Miller, J. (2008). Reconciling the roles: Reflections of an academic practitioner in TESOL (Australia). In A. Burns & J. Burton (Eds.), *Language teacher research in Australia and New Zealand* (pp. 149–164). Teachers of English to Speakers of Other Languages.

Moon, J. A. (2004). *Reflection in learning and professional development: Theory and practice*. Routledge.

Peeler, E. (2008). Open my eyes, reveal my blindness: Cultural awakening in teacher education (Australia). In A. Burns & J. Burton (Eds.), *Language teacher research in Australia and New Zealand* (pp. 165–180). Teachers of English to Speakers of Other Languages.

Ravelli, L. J., & Ellis, R. A. (Eds.). (2004). *Analyzing academic writing: Contextualized frameworks*. Continuum.

Richardson, L. (1990). *Writing strategies: Reaching diverse audiences*. Sage Publications.

Richardson, L. (1997). *Fields of play: Constructing an academic life*. Rutgers University Press.

Richardson, L. (2003). Writing: A method of inquiry. In N. K. Denzin & Y. S. Lincoln (Eds.), *Collecting and interpreting qualitative materials* (2nd ed.; pp. 499–541). Sage Publications.

Ricoeur, P. (1991). *A Ricoeur reader: Reflection and imagination* (M. J. Valdes, Ed.). University of Toronto Press.

Riessman, C. K. (1993). *Narrative analysis* (Qualitative Research Methods, Vol. 30). Sage Publications.

Schön, D. (1987). *Educating the reflective practitioner*. Jossey-Bass.

Shulman, L. S. (2004). Professional development: Learning from experience. In S. M. Wilson (Ed.), *The wisdom of practice: Essays on teaching, learning, and learning to teach* (pp. 521–544). Jossey-Bass.

Spellmeyer, K. (1998). A common ground: The essay in the academy. In V. Zamel & R. Spack (Eds.), *Negotiating academic literacies: Teaching and learning across languages and cultures* (pp. 105–122). Lawrence Erlbaum.

Stoynoff, S. (2004). Survey: Case studies in TESOL practice. *ELT Journal, 58*(4), 379–393.

Swales, J. (1990). *Genre analysis: English in academic and research settings*. Cambridge University Press.

Swales, J. (2004). *Research genres: Explorations and applications*. Cambridge University Press.

Wenger, E. (1998). *Communities of practice: Learning, meaning, and identity*. Cambridge University Press.

Winter, R., & Badley, G. (2007). Action research and academic writing: A conversation. *Educational Action Research, 15*, 2253–2270.

Zamel, V., & Spack, R. (Eds.). (1998). *Negotiating academic literacies: Teaching and learning across languages and cultures*. Lawrence Erlbaum.

CHAPTER 6

Patterns of Participation in Reflective Writing and Their Implications for Teacher Leadership Development

Joy Kreeft Peyton and Phil Quirke

As Cohen-Sayag and Fischl (2012) point out, the power of reflective writing, e.g., journal writing, is that it can mediate between existing and new knowledge, "breaking habitual ways of thinking, enhancing the development of metacognition, increasing awareness of tacit knowledge, facilitating self-exploration, and working out solutions to problems" (p. 21, citing Kerka, 2002, p. 1). We have seen this power demonstrated in the chapters of this book, which describe the use of reflective writing with in-service and pre-service teachers who are acting or developing as leaders, writing with supervisors, coaches, mentors, professors, and researchers who are helping to facilitate that leadership development.

This chapter describes patterns of reflective writing with teachers and prospective teachers, and those teaching and supporting them, and its impact on their leadership development, both in their teaching practices and throughout their teaching institutions. The majority of the data comes from the reflective writing of specific communities of teachers and teacher leaders in different countries of the world – Abu Dhabi, Austria, Brazil, Germany, Israel, Japan, Peru, and the United States – documented in a previous publication that the authors of this book edited and participated in: Burton, Quirke, Reichmann, and Peyton (2009). Data from an additional study (Cohen-Sayag & Fischl, 2012) are also included, because the study is relevant to our focus here. In our discussion, we examine teacher participation in and reactions to the reflective writing in which they engaged and their learning from it, as observed in their use of new knowledge and skills and changes in their teaching environments, with a focus on their leadership development. We then focus on the recent use of reflective writing to develop teacher leaders in a DREAM management course in Abu Dhabi, during the period 2016–2019 (see detailed discussion of the course in Chapter 2). As we describe in the conclusion, the patterns found in this review of writing in a wide range of contexts have implications for the use of reflective writing to promote leadership development in many different countries and educational contexts. There is also more work for all of us to engage in and much more to learn.

1 Documenting Patterns of Participation in and Outcomes of Reflective Writing of Current and Prospective Teachers and Teacher Leaders

As described in Chapter 1, we use Guskey's (2000) framework, Table 1.1 in Chapter 1, to review the patterns in and outcomes of reflective writing among the teachers with whom we have worked, in other publications that focus on this, and among the group of teachers that Phil Quirke has worked with over the past few years in the DREAM management course. In the following sections, we describe each of these in turn.

2 Participation Patterns

We have added *participation patterns* to Gusky's framework, because it is a critical component of any written interaction. Who contributes what? How often? In what ways? Who accesses and responds to what postings? Is there growth and development over time in the ways that individuals participate?

Studies of participation patterns in teachers' interactive writing have identified some interesting dynamics. For example, Carroll & Tatsuta (2009, p. 64), teacher educators who were both learning Chinese at a private conversation school in Japan (Michael Carroll, as a third language, through the medium of his second language, Japanese; Seiko Tatsuta, as a third language, through the medium of her first language, Chinese) wrote together for a year, in English, Japanese, and Chinese. They found that over time, their writing became more reflective, as they moved through the levels outlined by Burton (2005, 2009; see also the discussion in Chapter 1). They started with a focus on What happened? (a focus on events) and moved into How did it happen? Why did it happen?, and What does it mean? They argue (following Lipp, 2001; Carroll, 1994) that reflective writing for teachers learning a new language can be a way not only to focus on use of the language but also to reflect on their learning processes, even at low proficiency levels. They conclude that one powerful aspect of their written interactions was that they played dual roles as learners and enquirers into the teaching process, reflecting on multiple sides of the teaching/learning matrix.

Jeannot and Hunter (2009) held an online forum, on Blackboard, for two years in succession in a TESOL sociolinguistics course for prospective teachers, at a small university in the northwest United States. Each year, the participants included both non-native English speakers (from Taiwan, mainland China, Korea, and Japan) and native English speakers (from the United States).

The authors, who team-taught the class, are American and British. They found that participation patterns in the online forum were different from the in-class discussions. While many of the non-native English speakers did not participate in the oral, in-class discussions, they made 40% of the contributions to the written discussions, and their participation gave the sense that they had the chance to be experts with their native English-speaking peers. The authors also observed a willingness of students to share their understanding of concepts and to demonstrate their invention, or ownership, of theories that they had read about and discussed in class. They point out,

> The online forum, removed in space and time from the face-to-face encounter of the classroom, presents an opportunity not just for reflection but for self-expression, engagement, and even disagreement. After this experience, we would never consider teaching a seminar class without it. (p. 126)

Similarly, Trites (2009), in a graduate-level course, Applied Linguistics and Professional Practices, in the MA TESOL program in a university in the United States, found in the writing a strong sense that the participants were connecting with each other. Their journal entries (as well as oral feedback and course evaluations) indicated that they trusted each other and that each individual member of the group had benefited from the experiences of the others, a sense of reciprocity.

2.1 Participant Reactions

Participant reactions focus on what the participants believe about the written interactions and the ways that they are contributing to their learning and development. Do they find the interactions to be worthwhile? Are they contributing to their growth as teachers and leaders?

Using a systemic-functional approach (Halliday, 1994) and a critical discourse perspective (Fairclough, 1992), Reichmann (2009) analyzed the writing over a 15-month period of herself and a colleague, both teachers, and students in a Ph.D. program in Applied Linguistics in Brazil, in a course on written discourse analysis. She found changes in their reactions to each other and to the writing itself. One visible change was in their social relations, as they both discovered an increased sense of engagement and inclination to engage, with each other, with their students, and in their classes generally. They also both increased in their use of the grammatical subjects *we* and *let's* in their writing, indicating an increased sense of connection and symmetry between them.

Reichmann also found change in the ways that they both represented their activities in the classes they were teaching, moving from a focus on thinking (using "mental" verbs) to a focus on "creative doings" (p. 55). The colleague, in an email message written 18 months after their written interaction, summed up her reactions as a participant in this way:

> An interesting point is that the 'reflective written interaction' seems to enhance a deeper conception of the teacher's role in the teaching-learning process, and of the factors that contribute to this process. It is as if we were co-constructing, through writing, our own object of study: Our own pedagogical practice and our students' learning practice are foregrounded. Classroom reality becomes the focus of reflection, as opposed to isolated happenings. I remember that in the beginning of the DJ [dialogue journaling] I did not exactly know what I should be writing about. I portrayed isolated incidents, and seemed to be more worried about what I did (as if I could do anything by myself). Now I am more capable of enhancing student voice, although I still talk a lot ... Yesterday I was thinking how I really was trained as a teacher-researcher during the journal process. After all, my research projects are nothing more, nothing less than a sequel of our work; we really haven't stopped ... And I really appreciated your article (Reichmann, 2001); it is great to feel all this progress as a teacher, and that we accomplished this together. I really did not know what it meant to feel 'awareness' regarding pedagogical practice. And I don't have all those fears anymore. ... (pp. 55–56)

2.2   *Participant Learning*

Determining the types and levels of participant learning involves observing or interviewing participants or analyzing their writing and asking: What evidence is there that learning is taking place? Do we see teachers change over time in their views about language, their use of language, and themselves as teachers and current or potential leaders?

In interviews with teacher participants in Master's degree courses in Vienna, Austria, in which they engaged in freewriting (based on the work of Elbow, 1973), Mlynarczyk, Potzmann, and Haigner (2009) found that significant learning and changes in instructional approaches had taken place:

> Based on conversations with many program graduates years after completing the M.A., it seems clear that all of the teachers are changed to some extent by their participation. Teachers don't just walk away with a

new package of worksheets to copy for their students. Instead, they take away substantial ideas, concepts, and reflections that are deeply connected to their own personality and pedagogical values. (p. 134)

In analyzing the autobiographical writing of English teachers in a continuing education program in São Paulo, Brazil, Romero (2009) found evidence of learning in that the teachers began to write about their views of language, the learning process, influences on their learning, and how they felt about and performed their jobs at the time, as compared to earlier. She concludes, "The results achieved in the teacher education course I teach have reinforced the role of autobiography in critical reflection and its utmost importance for teachers' growth. A former student commented:

> Only when I wrote my autobiography did I understand who I really was as a professional and as a person. But, God, how difficult it was preparing it! But I loved it! I could finally see myself! And I was also surprised to be able to mentally see my former teachers again!" (p. 91)

Jeannot and Hunter (2009, described above) found that the discussions in which they engaged on Blackboard with their students provided an effective way to assess the participants' learning outcomes, because they were able to see when and how they were using the content covered in the course. Correa and Skibelski (2009) came to a similar conclusion in their writing with new teachers in São Paulo, Brazil.

2.3　*Participant Use of New Knowledge and Skills*

Discovering patterns of participants' use of new knowledge and skills in their teaching and development as leaders requires interviewing them orally or in written interactions, observing teacher lesson plans and classroom practices, or reviewing and reflecting on these together (Trites, Sroda, & Tseng, 2009).

Quirke and Zagallo (2009), in a teacher education course in Abu Dhabi, followed a semester of open-ended written discussion in dialogue journals between practicing teachers and their instructors with a set of questions for the teachers, which focused specifically on instructional approaches that they had discussed in their writing, and which the teachers responded to in writing:

– Can you give me an example of how you present in class through the use of stories?

- How do you set up your role plays?
- In what ways do you use music in your teaching?
- How do you help students develop their organizational skills? (p. 22)

They found that asking these questions of the teachers allowed them to start exploring the teachers' classroom approaches in depth and that the written interactions that followed the asking of these questions gave valuable information about what the teachers were applying in their instruction and gave the teachers opportunities to reflect in depth on their teaching and make changes to their approaches. They argue that "professional and profound change is only possible through introspection and reflection. ... By using reflective writing to understand individual narratives and how they impact teaching practices, teachers can become more rounded, confident, and effective teachers" (p. 13).

In a review of teachers' journals in a Master's degree program in Brazil, after they had engaged in written interaction, Reichmann (2009) found that teachers were creating new and more spaces in their lessons for reflection and dialogue among students and between the teacher and the students (p. 61).

Spencer (2009) found that when engaging in reflective writing when learning an additional language (in Japan, learning Japanese and in Germany, learning German), she was able to reflect on the experience of being both a language learner and a language teacher. This changed her relationship with her students, reducing the distance between herself and them, and resulted in her regarding and treating them as humans first and students second. It also created a classroom atmosphere of working together, with all members expressing and sharing their worries, ideas, and personalities.

After Cohen-Sayag and Fischl (2012) conducted a review of the research on outcomes of reflective writing in teachers' practice and found that no studies showed proven links between reflective writing and pre-service teachers' planning and teaching acts, they examined changes in the reflective writing of pre-service teachers with whom they worked during one year and connections to their level of teaching. They asked: "Will an ongoing process of writing a structured journal improve the pre-service teachers' reflective writing, in terms of numbers of explanations and higher levels of reflection?" (in line with Participant Learning, above) and "Will changes in reflective writing correlate with summative assessments of pre-service teachers' teaching practices?" (in line with Participant Use of New Knowledge and Skills). Study participants were 24 pre-service teachers in their third year of training in a special education program for primary and secondary schools in a teacher education college in Israel. The data were (for each teacher) a personal, structured reflective journal, submitted throughout the year, and the results of two classroom observations, at the end of the first and second semester. The pre-service teachers each wrote 8–10 monthly journals about a lesson they had planned and taught and submitted their journals to the supervisor once a month, from November to June. Supervisors responded to the journals: In one group (Group A), the supervisor wrote primarily confirmations and encouraging feedback; in the other group (Group B), the supervisor made comments, posed questions, wrote her own opinion, corrected students' writing, and suggested additional readings. As result of their analysis of the reflective writing, the authors came to three conclusions: (1) pre-service teachers need support and practice in reflective writing, or the writing may be unproductive, not leading to development of thinking or improved practice; (2) writers benefit from the kind of response that those in Group B received, with not only praise, but engagement in the topics that the participants were writing about; the teachers in Group B were involved as equals with their team members, discussing and implementing possibilities, acts, and goals; and (3) the involvement in reflective writing alone did not necessarily result in a change in teaching; the writers who engaged in critical thinking in their writing did show change in their teaching.

Cohen-Sayag and Fischl (2012) concluded that the context for reflective writing, the individuals involved, and the ways that they and supervisors engage in the writing together have an impact on the outcomes, in terms of participants' use of knowledge and skills in their teaching; and that this issue, impact of the writing on teaching behaviors (teaching acts), would benefit from more research.

2.4 Organization Change and Support

Documenting organization change and support for teachers and leaders involves observing and documenting instructional plans and foci in schools and teacher behavior in classes after teachers have participated in reflective writing. Observations that have been carried out have found that:

– Teachers engaged in reflective writing formed self-initiated writing groups, which they set up and implemented together, and they worked to promote the use of reflective writing in meaningful ways among the teachers in their school (Mlynarczyk, Potzmann, & Haigner, 2009, pp. 135–136).
– In one program, after a semester of reflective writing among some MA students/practicing teachers, an MA candidate stated that her 50 student teachers started writing in journals (Reichmann, 2009). The MA student

who reported this to Reichmann stated, "To say the least, the ripple effect triggered by journaling is fascinating" (p. 61).
– One school changed its culture, moving from maintaining lists of dos and don'ts for teachers to follow to promoting authentic dialogue among teachers and between teachers and supervisors, forming team teaching arrangements, starting service learning projects, and forming mentoring relationships (Salas, 2009, p. 155).

Jeannot and Hunter (2009) found that they, as team-teachers, as an unintended consequence of the Blackboard discussions that they facilitated, made changes to their pedagogical approaches in their classes, as they had ongoing opportunities in the online discussions to examine their teaching and to clarify their positions on critical issues in English teaching and teacher preparation.

2.5   *Student Learning*

Although studies of student and teacher or prospective teacher learning after they and their teachers or professors have engaged in reflective writing are limited, many teachers, after experiencing reflective writing themselves, have then introduced it to their students. Mlynarczyk, Potzmann, and Haigner (2009), in comparing texts written by grade 8 students in Austria, whose teachers had been involved in a reflective writing project, found that the students who had engaged in reflective writing wrote texts judged by the teachers to be superior in content, grammar, and syntax to the writing of grade 8 students who hadn't; wrote much more than asked to write by the teachers; and showed more interest in writing (p. 135).

Peyton et al. (1990) compared the writing of students in 6th grade learning English as a second language over a year's time on classroom essays and in dialogue journals, in which they wrote daily with their teacher. They found that over time, the students' dialogue journal writing became more and more complex, with richer vocabulary and more complex sentence and grammatical structures than their essay writing.

3   Participation Patterns and Outcomes of Teachers Developing as Leaders

The studies described above were carried out by a diverse group of teachers and scholars, with diverse groups of students, in many different contexts, and they focus on teachers and prospective teachers, although it is easy to see that the patterns described are also helpful with developing leaders. Here we focus on the work of Phil Quirke, who used reflective writing in DREAM Management courses, from 2016 to 2019, with the purpose of developing the participating teachers as leaders.

Between 2016 and 2019, three Introduction to DREAM Management courses were run with 32 participants from 11 countries; 11 from the United States, 6 from the United Kingdom (UK), 4 from the United Arab Emirates (UAE), 3 from other Arab countries, 3 from Africa, 2 from Canada, 2 from Ireland, and 1 from Russia. Participants had lived and worked in the UAE from 1 to 25 years, and the faculty held a variety of different leadership roles, from Program Chair to Campus Course Team Leader. This diverse multi-cultural group of experienced teacher educators (all faculty had graduate degrees with nine holding doctorates, and a minimum of three years school teaching and three years teacher education experience), general studies faculty, and English language teachers provided a rich kaleidoscope of past experiences that ensured lively discussion and contrastive reflective styles.

Chapter 2 describes the DREAM Management course in detail, so this section does not describe the course but focuses specifically on the participation patterns of the participants in reflective writing and how the DREAM Management approach to teacher leadership development empowered them to appreciate their strengths and build on the areas they identified as requiring further enhancement.

3.1   *Participation Patterns and Participant Reactions*

In the three DREAM Management courses run over the three years, discussion was offered within the Blackboard Learn LMS Discussion Board and through email. Interestingly, most participants preferred email, with one participant stating that the format

> was much easier, since the institution is so email dependent, being spread over the country and the 16 different campuses, meaning we always check our emails before anything else when we check in and therefore the discussion REPLY ALL contributions remain at the forefront of our tasks every day.

With few exceptions, every participant responded to each of the discussion forums focused on a DREAM principle once and in some detail, although the depth of response was clearly linked to the participant's situation and how relevant that principle was to the current challenges that they faced that week in the job. In the words of one participant, the consistency and depth of participant responses was due to "the discussion-based delivery of the content, which allowed us ... to synthesize ideas as we work through concepts". Other participants noted "the willingness of colleagues to engage honestly" and the "supportive, non-judgmental" nature of the forum, which was "not intimidating".

Interestingly, the reflective papers required at the end of each module constantly referenced the forum discussions and expanded on issues raised therein, demonstrating the growth and development of the participants. The final reflection also provided evidence of participant learning as they described which principle had most impacted their practice during the course:

> I liked the management-perspective of appraisal and delegation. Seeing that delegation is not just convenient but necessary for leaders and that properly delegating is a skill, I made an effort to delegate some work this semester, and I noticed that the working relationship with those people really developed. We became closer, I found that we engaged more, and work became more enjoyable because I wasn't so overtasked.

For one participant, it was clearly the overall reflective approach that impacted her learning in the course:

> DREAM is about having the Emotional Intelligence [EQ] to deal with your work life and those you work with. Although I have read articles about EQ and indeed discussed and addressed it in various courses and workshops I've delivered, DREAM gave me the chance to reflect on my EQ as well as think more deeply about how it affected me within my career.

3.2 *Participant Learning*

As noted in Chapter 2, each module of the DREAM Management course is structured around Quirke's model of Teacher Knowledge Development, with Knowledge Seeker readings and viewings followed by Knowledge Discusser email or discussion board forums and Knowledge User tasks. It concludes with a final module and a Knowledge Provider-referenced reflective paper. Unsurprisingly, the majority of examples exhibiting evidence of learning and change were drawn from the reflective papers submitted at the end of each module on a specific principle. Many of the reflections cited the articles from the readings, comments from the discussions, and details from the task experiences from the week as the participants attempted to use the new knowledge in context.

In some cases, the participant pointed to further learning and research triggered by the week's study and reflection, an indication of the cyclical nature of teacher knowledge development, as the Knowledge Provider reflection leads into new Knowledge Seeker research. An example of this is perfectly captured by a 2016 participant after the Recruit module:

> One area of interest for my professional development is to try and explore the complexity of the patterns of interaction in a blended interviewing environment where the candidate has to interact face-to-face with one or more interviewers, and through video conferencing devices with other interviewer(s).

In other cases, the learning was clearly demonstrated in a change in the participant's approach, as one academic coordinator noted in her reflection after the Delegate module:

> Before attending these classes, if I were asked about delegating at work, I certainly would have answered that I was a much happier person simply getting my work done, and that while at times this meant that I was overtasked and quite stressed, it also meant that I could control what was happening and how it was getting done.

Following the week's reading, discussion, and task, she concluded her reflection stating:

> I can see the value and the ease that it does bring into life, and definitely believe that it is something that I can continue to work on to help develop myself both professionally and personally.

Others commented on how the module had invigorated their practice and given it greater significance, as these extracts from one participant's reflection on the Enjoy principle demonstrate:

> I have to say that this week's DREAM Management content area, enjoyment and happiness, has been the most pleasurable, as this is something that interests me and an area which I choose to read about in my leisure

time. ... Reading the various articles on positivity and being happy in the workplace has had a positive impact on me, reinforcing and reminding me of the idea that I make my own happiness. ... After reading the articles, they had the effect of lifting me and put me in a positive frame of mind. I took this mindset into my classes. ... I have tried to keep a positive mindset in all situations and interactions, particularly this week. ... The focus on positivity and happiness has certainly lifted me this week and I feel it needs to be recognized and given emphasis in the workplace.

3.3 *Participant Use of New Knowledge and Skills*

The structure of the DREAM Management course requires that teachers think about "how our attitudes, beliefs, and assumptions are shaping our professional practice. As teachers, when we reflect on all the contextual variables that our teaching/learning environment involves, we are engaging in a long process that can empower all parties" including learners, in the words of one participant.

As noted above, the structure of the course required participants to use the new knowledge and skills as part of the task each week and apply it within their context before reflecting on the experience. Therefore, almost every reflection demonstrated participant application and use of the DREAM principle in question. For example, one participant noted in the Motivate module that

> The effort on my part to show appreciation really did go a long way in providing motivation to other people, in different ways and different motivations. I believe that strong relationships are the key to successful management, and by investing in the relationships with the people in our work and personal lives, we make 'managing' them and working with them much easier.

3.4 *Organization Change and Support*

Many participants commented on how the transparency and management focus of the course, in itself, was a demonstration of organizational change and support.

> It is the first time in my professional career where I have had a supervisor directly address the style of management that they use, and be very transparent about the way that they manage and the reasons why. ... This has made working for the establishment so much easier, as I am now working in an environment that is transparent, at least by my direct supervisor.

> DREAM management shouldn't be a Dream. It should be the standard, driven by the heart of the organization ... its people, collaboratively working towards a common accord.
>
> It didn't feel as though I was working on a course but doing my own research into a more positive and happy life!

This is a very human and up to date approach to management.

3.5 *Student Learning*

Many participants reflected not only on how the course impacted their leadership role but also how they took their principles into the classroom. One department chair took the discussion on Motivate to their department faculty professional development session and found that many of the teachers thought that the issues discussed occurred directly inside their classrooms as well, naming "lack of motivation from some students, little advancement in skill from some students, students' passive attitudes, the inability to get students to speak up, and difficulties getting students to take responsibility for their learning". This led to the discussion being extended to how teachers could use management techniques to improve student motivation, and some innovative projects were started to impact the classroom learning environments.

Under the Respect principle, one participant wrote the following:

> Showing respect to others applies to students, as well as other college staff and faculty. In class I am constantly referring to how to treat and work with children respectfully, as this needs to be modelled by the teacher and it is the behavior we want to see from children, both towards adults and their peers. One way to show that students are respected is by knowing their abilities, which applies in the college classroom as well as the child's classroom.

The reflection continued in detail about how the participant applied the Respect principle in her teaching and leadership and the impact that this has had on the young adult student teachers with whom she works.

A final example comes from a reflection on the Develop principle, where the participant drew an excellent parallel between the strategic planning process and the teacher's development of classroom rules.

> First, talking with the class about how they want to be treated by others, the importance of having rules (Ethos), then deciding collectively what those rules should be through collaboration (Vision), then providing examples of what those rules look like, sound like and act like (Strategy).

The rules aren't long and wordy, but clear, simple and concise phrases so that the students remember them and can explain what they mean in their own words.

4 Implications for Teacher Leadership Development

We hope that the power of written interaction in the many components of learning – from participants' participation to the learning that occurs and the impact on the educational enterprise overall – and its role in developing leaders is clear in this review of the research and description of the DREAM Management course. There are several implications that we can draw from the experiences described here.

4.1 Interactive Writing Provides New, Often More In-Depth Communication Experiences

While reading and writing are understood to influence each other, the power of reading in an interactive experience, with fellow teacher/learners and coaches/mentors, and its influence on writing, is not often considered. However, Phil Quirke's students found that the reading and writing that they did in the interactive forums played a powerful role in the reflective texts that they wrote at the end of each module.

We often consider interaction to be oral and want students to participate orally in class discussions. Some authors cited here found that students who did not participate in oral discussions in class (often non-native speakers of the language) were engaged and active in the interactive writing. Jeannot and Hunter (2009) found that writing in an online forum presented an opportunity for the students "not just for reflection but for self-expression, engagement, and even disagreement" (p. 126). They claim that these activities would not have occurred if the students were not interacting and reflecting in writing.

4.2 The Context for the Writing Makes a Difference

Many of the authors cited here point out that the writing patterns and outcomes depend to a great extent on the context in which the writing is done and the expectations of and guidance from the mentor, coach, or professor. The writing may be barely reflective at all (e.g., diaries of daily activities), it may be done in learning logs (more reflective), or it may be highly introspective and analytical (most reflective).

In the writing of Quirke's students, we see that the structure of the DREAM Management course required the participants to reflect on their experience of applying new knowledge in context, and the organization of the DREAM principles and related readings resulted in increased depth of reflection over time. The responses of the tutor to their reflective paper submissions, and the responses of their colleagues to their reflections and contributions to the discussion forums, also had an impact on the depth and the detail of their reflective writing as the course progressed.

4.3   The Writing Is More Powerful When Connected to a Class or Leadership Activity

Trites (2009) found that discussing topics in class about which participants are writing in journals helps them see the value of the writing. If the topics are never mentioned in class, teachers may see the writing as a completely ancillary, unrelated activity, and a waste of their time. This was also echoed in the structure of the DREAM Management course, which required both discussion and reflection on each principle, so that participants clearly linked the learning from the discussion forums to their later reflective writing and to the leadership work they were engaged in.

4.4   The Participation of the Coach, Mentor, or Professor Can Have an Impact

Jeannot and Hunter (2009) believe and found, in their online discussions with students on Blackboard, that the quality of participation changes when instructors take part.

> In both courses, our postings accounted for about one-fifth of the total postings. Colleagues who use Blackboard but do not post themselves report that not only the quantity but also the quality of postings begins to diminish, with postings becoming increasingly off topic and less well thought out. We believe that if the online forum is to be used to good effect as a reflective writing forum, it needs to be done with careful, but not overbearing, instructor participation and moderation, a point that mirrors our thoughts regarding in-classroom instruction as well. (p. 122)

The coach, mentor, or professor can be a facilitator, and also a learner, as we have seen in examples in this chapter. The participants in the DREAM management course seemed to have a strong sense of community, working in collaboration with the professor, even in terms of developing evaluated works (the end-of-module reflective essays).

We conclude, therefore, that reflective writing is most impactful when it is collaborative, contextualized, connected, and carefully facilitated. Teachers as current and prospective leaders need to see that there is value in reflecting in depth together on issues and theories that are relevant to their local context and their current and future work. They can then experience the power of learning that should be the outcome of well-designed and facilitated reflective discussions.

References

Burton, J. (2005). The importance of teachers writing on TESOL. *TESL-EJ, 9*(2), 1–18. http://tesl-ej.org/ej34/a2.pdf

Burton, J. (2009). Reflective writing – Getting to the heart of teaching and learning. In J. Burton, P. Quirke, C. Reichmann, & J. K. Peyton (Eds.), *Reflective writing: A way to lifelong teacher learning* (pp. 1–11). TESL-EJ, E-Book Edition. http://tesl-ej.org/books/reflective_writing.pdf

Burton, J., Quirke, P., Reichmann, C., & Peyton, J. K. (2009). (Eds.). *Reflective writing: A way to lifelong teacher learning.* TESL-EJ, E-Book Edition. http://tesl-ej.org/books/reflective_writing.pdf

Carroll, M. (1994). Teacher-learner negotiation in continuing curriculum development: A case study. In J. Burton (Ed.), *Perspectives on the classroom* (CALUSA Research on Language and Learning Series 1; pp. 134–152). CALUSA, University of South Australia.

Carroll, M., & Tatsuta, S. (2009). Collaborative reflections on learning another language: Implications for teaching. In J. Burton, P. Quirke, C. Reichmann, & J. K. Peyton (Eds.), *Reflective writing: A way to lifelong teacher learning* (pp. 63–71). TESL-EJ, E-Book Edition. http://tesl-ej.org/books/reflective_writing.pdf

Cohen-Sayag, E., & Fischl, D. (2012). Reflective writing in pre-service teachers' teaching: What does it promote? *Australian Journal of Teacher Education, 37*(10), 20–36.

Correa, D., & Skibelski, D. (2009). Online dialogue journals – A virtual voice. In J. Burton, P. Quirke, C. Reichmann, & J. K. Peyton (Eds.), *Reflective writing: A way to lifelong teacher learning* (pp. 96–110). TESL-EJ, E-Book Edition. http://tesl-ej.org/books/reflective_writing.pdf

Elbow, P. (1973). *Writing without teachers.* Oxford University Press.

Fairclough, N. (1992). *Discourse and social change.* Polity Press.

Guskey, T. (2000). *Evaluating professional development.* Corwin Press.

Halliday, M. A. K. (1994). *An introduction to functional grammar* (2nd ed.). Edward Arnold.

Jeannot, M., & Hunter, J. (2009). The discussion doesn't end here – The online discussion board as a reflective writing forum. In J. Burton, P. Quirke, C. Reichmann, & J. K. Peyton (Eds.), *Reflective writing: A way to lifelong teacher learning* (pp. 111–127). TESL-EJ, E-Book Edition. http://tesl-ej.org/books/reflective_writing.pdf

Kerka, S. (2002). Journal writing as an adult learning tool. *Practice Application Brief No. 22.* http://www.cete.org/acve/docgen.asp?tbl=pab&ID=112

Lipp, E. (2001). Building a cross-cultural community of learners and writers through pen-pal journals. In J. Burton & M. Carroll (Eds.), *Journal writing* (pp. 113–124). TESOL Publications.

Mlynarczyk, R., Potzmann, R., & Haigner, K. (2009). The role of freewriting in teachers' growth and development: Insights from Austria. In J. Burton, P. Quirke, C. Reichmann, & J. K. Peyton (Eds.), *Reflective writing: A way to lifelong teacher learning* (pp. 128–142). TESL-EJ, E-Book Edition. http://tesl-ej.org/books/reflective_writing.pdf

Peyton, J. K., Staton, J., Richardson, G., & Wolfram, W. (1990). The influence of writing task on ESL students' written production. *Research in the Teaching of English, 24*(2), 142–171.

Quirke, P., & Zagallo, E. (2009). Moving towards truly reflective writing. In J. Burton, P. Quirke, C. Reichmann, & J. K. Peyton (Eds.), *Reflective writing: A way to lifelong teacher learning* (pp. 12–30). TESL-EJ, E-Book Edition. http://tesl-ej.org/books/reflective_writing.pdf

Reichmann, C. L. (2001). Teachers-in-dialogue: Exploring practice in an interactive professional journal. In J. Burton & M. Carroll (Eds.), *Journal writing* (pp. 125–135). TESOL.

Reichmann, C. (2009). Constructing communities of practice through memoirs and journals. In J. Burton, P. Quirke, C. Reichmann, & J. K. Peyton (Eds.), *Reflective writing: A way to lifelong teacher learning* (pp. 49–62). TESL-EJ, E-Book Edition. http://tesl-ej.org/books/reflective_writing.pdf

Romero, T. R. S. (2009). Reflecting through autobiographies in teacher education. In J. Burton, P. Quirke, C. Reichmann, & J. K. Peyton (Eds.), *Reflective writing: A way to lifelong teacher learning* (pp. 82–95). TESL-EJ, E-Book Edition. http://tesl-ej.org/books/reflective_writing.pdf

Salas, S. (2009). Teaching on soft earth – Writing and professional transformations in Peru. In J. Burton, P. Quirke, C. Reichmann, & J. K. Peyton (Eds.), *Reflective writing: A way to lifelong teacher learning* (pp. 143–155). TESL-EJ, E-Book Edition. http://tesl-ej.org/books/reflective_writing.pdf

Spencer, S. A. (2009). The language teacher as language learner. In J. Burton, P. Quirke, C. Reichmann, & J. K. Peyton (Eds.), *Reflective writing: A way to lifelong teacher learning* (pp. 31–48). TESL-EJ, E-Book Edition. http://tesl-ej.org/books/reflective_writing.pdf

Trites, L. (2009). Small-group journals as a tool of critical reflection: A measure of success and failure. In J. Burton, P. Quirke, C. Reichmann, & J. K. Peyton (Eds.), *Reflective writing: A way to lifelong teacher learning* (pp. 72–81). TESL-EJ, E-Book Edition. http://tesl-ej.org/books/reflective_writing.pdf

Trites, L., Sroda, M. S., & Tseng, J. M. (2009). *Multi-dimensional co-teaching/mentoring model for on-the-job teacher training.* Unpublished manuscript.

CHAPTER 7

Reflective Writing to Develop Teacher Leaders: Where to Go from Here

Phil Quirke, Joy Kreeft Peyton, Jill Burton, Carla Reichmann and Latricia Trites

1   Reflections on Developing Teachers as Leaders

As we have seen in the chapters in this book, classroom teachers can play many different leadership roles, each carrying considerable responsibility for their own learning as well as that of others. They can serve as classroom teachers, teacher researchers, team leaders, coaches, mentors, program managers, and teacher educators in professional development settings and in tertiary programs. However, those who are expected to be leaders (program, school, and university managers) are often following directions and implementing educational reforms designed by others. Frequently, they must rely on their own insights. Often professionally isolated, not all may consider themselves to also be learners who can learn from others, such as teachers and teacher educators. An inclusive, collaborative leadership environment can draw and build on the strengths of managers, curriculum specialists, and teachers. This book is focused on those professionals who, while primarily teachers, can envisage leading roles for themselves, whether in classrooms or administrative offices.

Unfortunately, through no fault of their own, learners as prospective teachers and qualified practicing teachers, who are temporarily formal students again in in-service settings and postgraduate programs, often come to perceive leadership as a management hierarchy that reinforces divisions between teaching and managing and overlooks the potential for all members of the teaching profession to take leading roles. Moreover, there is currently little recognition in or outside the profession when teachers try leading from the classroom. This division is further entrenched by the numerous competing requirements of teachers. Many teachers, therefore, believe that the only way to fulfill guiding and leading roles in the profession is to leave the classroom and become managers themselves. But administrative management tends to have its own directives and discourse, which may encourage other teachers to decide that leading is not part of what they do.

In reality, leadership is involved in all facets of learning and teaching. Learners have a strong role to play in their own development, and teachers help to make this happen. Teachers who are leaders are effective learners themselves and model lifelong learning and responsibility.

'Being a learner', always 'becoming', offers a different mindset on leadership from traditional management and instruction, one that is more closely aligned with current social constructivist models of learning and teaching (e.g., Louden, 1991; Sharkey & Johnson, 2003; Wells & Chang-Wells, 1992). These articulate the intentions to be open, to share what you think and (believe you) know, and to hear and see what others have to say. They are concerned with much more than facilitating, because they are premised on sharing and collaboration, which we in this book would argue are the key qualities of authentic leadership and responsible action that underpin authority and voice.

2   The Role of Reflective Writing in Leadership Development

Reflective writing, in all of its different forms, is a powerful means of helping teachers develop as leaders and can lead to significant personal professional growth as they examine and write about their teaching and about themselves as teachers who, as learners as well, can influence the profession. It is a flexible resource for all learners, and particularly for teachers as leaders. It offers thinking frameworks based on disciplined, searching questions, which help inquiring teachers build and continue building their understanding of teaching and leadership. It supports every stage of teachers functioning as professionals who are also effective leaders: planning, implementing, inspiring, and evaluating are embedded in every professional activity that has to do with teaching.

Teachers as leaders who write reflectively begin by observing, then examining, questioning, and sharing perspectives on their and their students' and fellow teachers' use and development of language; ways of learning; pedagogical approaches; and attitudes about teaching, learning, and leading endeavors. Teachers functioning in this way employ reflective writing to move their thinking from a focus on events, that is 'What happened?' to 'How did it happen?' 'Why did it happen?' and 'What do these events mean?' As teachers continue to think and write over time, significant identity construction as teaching professionals can take place.

Some professors using interactive writing with prospective teachers have found that those who speak very little in class open up and engage with others in journals, blogs, and other forms of written interaction. The same holds true with teachers in in-service professional development programs. Some participants have found that the written interactions result in stronger connections and a sense of community among members of a class and the teacher (Chapters 2 and 5 illustrate this). Some have found that rather than simply learning a set of facts, learners come out of the reflective writing opportunity with ideas, concepts, and reflections that are deeply connected to their own personality, pedagogical values, and leadership beliefs (these developments underlie Chapters 3 and 4). Chapter 6 demonstrates the wide range of professional growth that can happen over time in settings where reflective engagement with teaching is encouraged. In all of these cases, teachers become deeply involved in the content they are encountering. These sorts of professional environments are vital if teachers are to develop as the leaders the profession needs. Although this approach appears to increase responsibilities for already overworked teachers, it nourishes their self-respect and their professional motivations. It supports them to be the profession's writers, inscribers, and reifiers – which they should and often want to be. It is primarily through the written word that a profession is understood in the community and in academe and can support deep reflection and renewal. It is essential that teachers be listened to, respected, and embraced as leaders and, where it is possible, that they speak up.

However, many teachers are not accustomed to engaging in reflective writing, alone, with others, or for others; and many see it as a burden when they already have enough to do. Writing about teaching becomes just another required task in a long list, to be checked off. They also may not experience or recognize the patterns of growth described in this and the preceding chapters. They need support and guidance as they practice and engage in this type of writing because it is likely new to them, something not even encountered when they were school learners themselves.

Immersion in reflective writing experiences might include teachers writing reflectively about an educational experience, starting with a narrative description of what was involved, followed by an analysis of any critical incidents (e.g., Tripp, 1993), triggered by the initial descriptive reflections. In essence, the teachers as writers would turn from description to considering the relationships between the task and the incidents described to characterize their management and their relation to leadership, as in any one of the units explicated in the DREAM model in Chapter 2, resulting in each teacher's emerging educational leadership philosophies.

Class leaders – tutors, professors, mentors, coaches, and supervisors – and their participants as colleagues can respond to reflections during any class or course, because there will be written records of them, and can construct continuing productive discussions about leadership development. These might include making comments, asking questions, writing their own opinions and reflections on colleagues' reflective writing, and suggesting additional readings (as happened in teacher research group meetings in Chapter 5). Questions asked in supportive, reflective settings can help teachers and prospective teachers deconstruct the issues they are working with in teaching situations.

Reflective writing activities might also include organized writing around specific topics (such as those focused on in class) or principles (as is done with the DREAM Management approach described in Chapter 2). As stated in Chapter 6, reflective writing is most effective when it is collaborative, contextualized, connected, and carefully facilitated.

Teachers who are knowledge builders and emerging leaders can function in a state of continual becoming, because there is sufficient stability in what is recorded, written, and shared that they can trust each other enough to risk being creative. Trust stimulates communities of practice (Wenger, 1998) in which participants can share insights from their individual contexts in a collaborative environment. The community relationship is one of mutuality, complementarity, reciprocity, collaboration, interdependence – and independence. In addition, communities of practice can push each participant beyond their immediate comfort zones.

3 Reflecting on the Chapters in This Book: Raising Questions

Each chapter in this book describes different uses of reflective writing; with different groups of teachers, learners, and leaders; in very different contexts. Here we reflect on what we have learned from writing these chapters and some questions that they raise for teachers to consider.

3.1   *Chapter 1: Reflective Writing and Its Potential for Developing Teacher Leaders*

This chapter surveys the many ways that leadership is considered in the profession of teaching language learners. It emphasizes what can happen in the classroom for the teacher who orchestrates learning with learning, and not directing, at the forefront. The chapter reviews strategies that have been developed over the years to support learners, teachers, teacher learners, teacher educators, and teacher researchers.

Questions:
– In what additional ways can reflective, interactive writing be used to develop this population of educators?
– Are there ways that they, and we, can go even deeper than we have in the articles and contexts described?

3.2 Chapter 2: An Approach to Using Reflective Writing to Develop Teacher Leaders: DREAM Management

This chapter explores and exemplifies the key features and benefits of reflective writing through DREAM, a framework that has become a development program for all teaching professionals involved in any kind of leadership role in a national, higher education setting, and it has spread well beyond its initial settings. The discussion shows the role of reflective writing in communicative encounters as a richly productive, rewarding activity.

Questions:
- What kinds of leaders are being supported in the context described here? How?
- What is the author's leadership role? Does it model the principles being covered?
- What are additional activities that this group of professionals might engage in and questions that they might ask?

3.3 Chapter 3: Mentoring Reflection: Teaching Pre-Service Teachers to Ask Why

In the context described, the chapter reveals how difficult reflective writing can be and addresses the practical issues involved in creating the time required for effective reflection. In addition, it reveals that while many supervisors, mentors, and teachers assume that their mentees are able to reflect naturally, this is most often not the case. A key constraint is the lack of institutional recognition of the time and effort involved and of those who engage in it, which leads to questions regarding how teachers can be given more opportunities for leadership development as curriculum innovators and teacher researchers.

Questions:
- What leadership role does Latricia, the author, have?
- Is she working in isolation?
- How can she create the time and freedom required to deepen the level of reflective writing that is done?
- What kinds of leaders are being supported? And how?
- How can reflective writing be used as the central tool she values in teacher education programs?

3.4 Chapter 4: Co-leadership through Dialogue and Reflective Writing in the Teaching Practicum

This chapter describes the complexity and intricacy of setting up and implementing a specialized, cross-institutional teaching program and portrays vividly the role that dialogic reflection played in how the program functioned as a learning tool that gave all participants voice, and thereby an element of leadership.

Questions:
- What did leadership mean for the author as the supervisor, for the cooperating teacher (CT), and for the student teachers (STS)?
- Did the supervisor, the CT, and the STS have different expectations?
- Did the CT and the STS see themselves in leading roles of any kind? Where, when and how?
- What kinds of leaders were being supported in this context?
- How was Carla, the author, leading in this new approach to the teaching practicum, and how did Carla and Rachel work together as co-leaders?
- How could the writing experiences described in this chapter be exploited to promote further learning and leadership development for all of the participants?

3.5 Chapter 5: Visions and Realities: Doctoral Perspectives on Practice and Leadership

For the teachers described in this chapter to perform as leaders in their usual teaching contexts means that they take responsibility for their learning and develop voice, both critical issues at the doctoral level. That doctoral students can write authoritatively and, at the same time, authentically, cannot be assumed, and is actually rare. These (potentially conflicting) skills and qualities have to be learned and cultivated, which may be culturally challenging.

Teachers as doctoral graduates are expected to publish and to promote their profession and teaching knowledge within and outside professional, academic, and community contexts. Many doctoral programs now include refereed publications as a requirement for graduation. Reflective writing, a versatile tool, can be oriented toward the classroom, academia, or the community, and it can be rigorous, systematic, and disciplined.

Questions:
- What leadership roles do postgraduate students need to explore as they develop their professional writing?
- What leadership roles do postgraduate students, as practicing teachers, already have on entry to postgraduate programs? How can these be further developed as part of their studies?
- How can leadership discussions and reflections enhance research processes in teaching contexts?
- How might communities of practice be formed in other teacher education contexts for teachers as potential leaders?

3.6 Chapter 6: *Patterns of Participation in Reflective Writing and Their Implications for Leadership Development*

This chapter describes the ways that patterns of participation can be examined in the reflective writing that teachers engage in and the impact that it can have on their teaching and leadership development. By studying these participation patterns and considering who contributes what, how often, and in what ways, we can gain insights into who leads reflective discussions and what leadership qualities and characteristics are being displayed in their writing. Drawing attention to these features and asking participants to further review who accesses and responds to what postings can encourage growth and development over time in the depth of reflective writing and the ways that teachers participate in reflective discussions.

Questions:
- What does this chapter suggest about the nature of leadership in teaching, in what ways, and in what settings?
- What does it suggest for teachers about future directions for leadership development through reflective writing?

4 Implications for Written Reflective Inquiry in Teacher Leadership Education

This section outlines strategies for readers to explore further, in their own settings, the roles, challenges, and complexities of writing reflectively to promote leadership development. It also suggests some approaches to reflective writing that might be investigated. We are not suggesting that you attempt all of them, or all at once! Just the ones that appeal to you in your teaching and institutional situations. You could take several, for example, and create an initial sequence of steps to follow:

- Write with teacher colleagues, especially when teaching the same course in different classes in a semester.
- Form equal partnerships with others involved in the class – cooperating co-teachers, tutors, or co-trainers – and create an atmosphere of comradeship and cohesive collectives.
- Have participants in classes form reflective writing groups (communities of practice), in which they can develop confidence to write openly and transparently with each other.
- Help teachers understand and grow to experience reflective writing as a natural habit that they can perform regularly, something that becomes part of their identity and personal growth.

- Ask questions that stimulate analysis, moving from describing what you are reading, to reflecting on its impact on you. 'How' and 'Why' questions, which promote deeper exploration and reflection, will be helpful here.
- Provide guidance and direction on how to increase depth of thinking in regular writing sessions in which everyone is engaged in written reflection, including yourself.
- Encourage participants to connect practical experiences with pedagogic and leadership theories. In this way, you are modeling the types of interactions that promote increased depth of reflection and changes in instructional practice that they can use in their own situations.
- Consider the importance of 'listening' in reflective writing and have participants explicitly reflect on the concept of noticing what others are writing.
- Be open yourself to being asked 'Why' and 'How' questions by others.
- Encourage participants to reflect on their writing over time: For example, is it moving from 'What happened?' to deeper reflections, demonstrating 'Why did it happen?' and considering 'What are our views on this?' 'Are there other views to take into account?' 'What else might we think about and pursue?'
- Ask participants to review their reflective writing from earlier and, for example, in pairs or small groups, reflect collaboratively to provide constructive feedback on each other's reflections. The aim is for participants to reflect on their earlier writing in light of subsequent experiences, re-examine their initial theorizing in the context of these intervening events, and question how their perspectives may have changed and may change further when thinking about future development.
- Promote intentionality and focus in reflective writing: that is, look at the focus of the activity that is being examined and the purpose of reflecting on it. Consider what questions and techniques you can use to encourage participants to write regularly in ways that deepen, but also focus and concentrate, their thinking and explorations. Model these processes in your own reflective contributions.

5 Types of Leadership

It will be evident from reading this book that leadership is an elastic, complex concept, which eludes easy definition because of its many diverse manifestations and alternative labels. Each of the chapters in this book offers nuanced interpretations of how teachers become leaders or encounter leadership challenges, and how individuals are managed or guided to reach their full potential.

There is not a great deal written on leadership for teachers. Discussions of leadership have largely adopted terms and concepts from business and administrative sectors of government. Other professions, such as law, engineering, and medicine have not established the management systems experienced in teaching. They don't seem to need them. Even though those professions have explicit standards and gatekeeping procedures, their operating systems remain relatively lean, allowing professionals in the workplace freedoms that teachers often don't seem to have or recognize.

Sports, perhaps, provide some relevant terms and concepts for the teaching environment. Successful teams usually have good coaches, who, working from behind, build up players' confidence through focusing on each team member's unique potential, pushing members who are ready and nurturing those who are less confident. Coaches focus on building trust, on developing self-respect and motivation, and, ultimately, on fulfilment for all team members alongside achievement of team goals. New team members expect to join a team with its own established ethos and goals. Coaches are strong leaders. Though they are not current players, they have been and so have credibility in players' eyes. They are often the bridge, a buffer, even, between the players and management and sponsors. A central role for coaches is inspiring their teams to aim high, having the creative skills and vision to look ahead. They are essential resources in all of these ways, and at the same time resource full. They are often the leaders of a team, as much as the team's captain, who may not be in place long. This elaborated metaphor may shed light on how the teaching profession could address notions of leadership that teachers, as well as the administrative managers in the background, could embrace. Coaching is a more assertive mode of leadership than mentoring, which emphasizes the nurturing aspect of leadership and sees the relationship as a partnership, with a duality of reflective learning (as described in Chapter 3). Distinguishing between coaching and mentoring highlights the contribution that each role plays in professional development and leadership – and also the slipperiness involved in defining leadership roles.

The prevalent term for leaders in teaching at present is 'manager'. Yet it is ambiguous, so it is another somewhat unhelpful, term. You can manage in the sense of 'coping', or 'getting by', or you can be directive, in control, and responsible for others. In this book, we have focused on the term 'leaders', envisaging teachers as leaders in all the complex, diverse ways we have portrayed, each of which entails responsibility for learning and teaching. We think it is a more inclusive, constructive term, which offers ways forward for all teachers to have the satisfaction of contributing to how their profession develops. After all, in the teaching profession as teachers, we are all involved in learning and in modeling learning – in education, in its original sense of 'leading out', bringing out the full potential in our students, colleagues, and, most of all, ourselves.

Thus, in the next section, we talk about what the projects and writings in the preceding chapters have meant to each of us and where they are leading us next.

6 Next Steps for the Authors of This Book

We, the five authors of this book, are inspired by the possibilities described here, and we plan to continue to move forward together. Here are some of our plans.

6.1 Phil Quirke

I plan to persuade my co-authors and other members of our loose international 'reflective writing on reflective writing' group to join me in a collaborative exploration of our exchanges, discussions, and reflective writing over the past two decades, since many of us came together as contributors to Jill Burton and Michael Carroll's edited volume, *Journal Writing* (2001). I have all of these saved, and I would love to see the learning and reflection that we would generate through an in-depth exploration of these earlier reflections, using Burton's reflective writing typology (2005, 2009) at a level 5 by asking ourselves:
– Are these earlier reflections still credible?
– Are they still reasonable?
– Why? Why not?
– What do these earlier reflections mean now in light of our subsequent experiences?

The description of this level states that "after longer intervals, writers use the developing spiral of reflection to re-examine initial theorizing in light of intervening events that may have changed their perspectives" (see Type 5 Comments in Table 1.2 in Chapter 1). The nearly two decades since our initial reflections is definitely the longest interval I will have experienced when looking back at earlier reflections. Even the 11 years since our last publication together (Burton, Quirke, Reichmann, & Peyton, 2009) is longer than any in-depth analysis or interpretative review I have made on my earlier writing, so I approach this with some trepidation, but more excitement. Our reflective writing group has always been so refreshing and important to me. It is international and is based on a passion for teaching and learning and sharing knowledge, unrestricted by boundaries and egos. It stands against the corporatization we see happening in academia. It is a meeting of minds but just as importantly, a meeting of hearts. I would, therefore, like to take advantage of this book to ask my colleagues here and now if they are interested in joining me on this reflective journey and continuing to work together.

My second plan is to continue working on the development of the DREAM Management courses and make them available to a far wider audience by launching them as self-study online modules and courses through one of the available online platforms, such as Moodle, Google Classroom, or Blackboard Open. I plan to reflect in depth on how the courses can continue to ensure the reflective requirements, and how I can provide a structure for these participant reflections and constructive feedback in new ways that continue to encourage increasing depth of reflection.

6.2   *Joy Peyton*

I have been fascinated by and engaged in dialogue journal writing since the 1980s, when I worked with Jana Staton, Roger Shuy, and a 6th grade teacher in California to study, analyze, and describe her writing in dialogue journals with 26 students each day throughout the school year and document the students' development as English language users and writers. In collaboration with Jana Staton, I continue to build the article about dialogue journal writing on Wikipedia,[1] and we plan to add an online space where teachers, teacher leaders, and students can engage in reflective writing online. I am very grateful for the opportunity to collaborate with my co-authors here, and I look forward to their engagement in this initiative.

6.3   *Jill Burton*

I would love us to explore Phil's suggestion further, to examine the archive of our communications over the years. What foresight that was! Whatever we do, or don't do, I for one am so grateful that none of our writings and exchanges have been lost. A collaborative project that looks for meaning in what we have collectively written and where it could still take us, as Phil has suggested, could be a fabulous next direction, spiralling onwards.

Coincidentally, I've used the spiral concept myself. I see a spiral as a circle (e.g., a cycle of inquiry or of action research) that has opened out to potentially endless looping. It can go sideways, backwards, make big or small loops; once begun it can spiral forever (see Burton, 2000, p. 13).

Apart from these enduring interests, I am fascinated by biography and all of its variant forms – memoir, bio-fiction, creative non-fiction, letters, diaries – processes that embed learning in experience – and I now try to apply these narrative tools in all of my own work and the work that we engage in together. Writing is what I do. It is who I am, how I learn, how I become. Writing is what gives me agency and purpose. It gives me *why*.

6.4 Carla Reichman

Involved with letter writing and journaling since a young age, during my Masters degree program at the School for International Training in Brattleboro, Vermont in the early 90s, I came across reflective journaling as a learning-teaching tool in schools and academia. My PhD research involved dialogue journaling, and during this period, I came across Joy Peyton's and Jill Burton's work. Journals have been part of my teacher research practice ever since, as well as teacher and learner narratives, autobiographies, photobiographies, reflective blogs, portfolios, and internship reflections. Being part of the *Reflective Writing* book (Burton, Quirke, Reichmann, & Peyton, 2009) and then also part of the discussion group that followed has been an incredible learning experience. On more than one occasion, the professional support I have received from this group has been crucial. Spanning decades, Phil's archive is a jewel, and the challenge is wonderful.

I love writing, I love teaching, and I love the ongoing dialogue with learners and teachers – in good times and hard times, such as our current 'new normal', wherever this will lead us. I hope to explore new narrative possibilities in the supervised internship, for example, in whatever format, remotely or face to face, when schools and universities reopen in Northeast Brazil.

6.5 Latricia Trites

I began using student journaling when it was *en vogue* in the mid 1980s. Admittedly, I used it quite ineffectively, yet was reflective enough to realize my folly. I abandoned the practice until I was able to develop a stronger understanding of the importance of dialogue in journaling. When I embarked on revising my implementation of classroom reflective, dialogue journaling, as chronicled in our first collaborative publication (Trites, 2001), I became aware of how much students needed direct, focused instruction on exactly how to be reflective.

Throughout the years, I have worked to instill quality reflective practices in my students; however, moving forward I hope to develop a reflective mentoring protocol that can be implemented throughout our teacher education program. I plan to develop modules that could be adopted by teacher trainers, university supervisors, and administrators so that not only pre-service teachers (PTs), but also cooperating teachers (CTs) can develop a better understanding of the role of reflection in the mentoring process.

7   Reflective Writing and Teachers as Leaders – Next Steps for Us and the Field

All reflective, professional activities in teaching and teacher education have the potential to engage individuals in becoming leaders. Reflective practices encourage teachers to consider themselves as lifelong learners who are ultimately responsible for their own development, the learning of their students, and collaboration with others they work and connect with in the arenas that make sense for them. We learn a great deal, from ourselves and each other, when we engage in these activities together, and this book is living proof of the power of purposeful, focused reflective writing to impact the lives and careers of all of us who have been involved in this wonderful group.

As a group, we five exhibit many of the features of a Community of Practice (see Wenger, 1998): flexible participation and writing and publishing together, individually and with others (reification). We practice situated learning: Each of us works in several diverse, specific settings, though our professional reach is global. Whatever the individual professional contexts for our writing reflectively, the tenor of how we work together confirms the social-situated nature of learning. Thus, the Community of Practice concept is a constructive frame for understanding how we work together and for our suggesting it as a supportive frame for other teacher educators and teachers as leaders.

As far as the chapters in this book are concerned, Carla's and Latricia's work in Chapters 3 and 4 can be read as descriptions of professional learning communities of practice, as can Jill's in Chapter 5. These, while unique, are also typical of contexts in which the majority of English language teachers learn teaching and leading; they reflect the social constructivist nature of how we learn, teach and lead, and publish. On a macro level, Phil, in Chapter 2, examines the sorts of professional knowledge constructions that can go on in national-level organizations. In his DREAM project, teachers as leaders participate from a range of regional settings within one national higher-education institution. Participants represent their own knowledge-building clusters, each of which is networked into the overarching organizational structure, forming what Wenger-Trayner et al. (2015) have called landscapes of practice. This metaphor encourages reflections on the boundaries between such landscapes, which can be established or demolished as the clusters construct meaningful practice-based development together. Chapter 5, with its teacher-researcher group (TRG) is a another example of a landscape of practice, which formed a socio-professional learning community in one location around international doctoral learners from many different countries and backgrounds, with each participant representing localized professional conditions.

As we bring this book to a close in the current lockdown around the world, and as we have experienced the past several months in a virtual universe of online teaching, teacher education, and learning, we conclude by raising the question of whether we will ever go back to the professional life in which we participated before, on campus or at school. The world of education has been revolutionized in recent months and will never be the same again. Teaching and learning have taken place; most professionals, from Kindergarten classes to postgraduate education, have adapted quickly and effectively to the new technologies and ways of communicating with their students; and most students have been just as adaptable, if not more so. However, there are concerns, especially for students in the early years and those with special needs. Many teachers and faculty have felt the strain of coming to terms with the new teaching medium while also supporting their children's online learning. How does a higher education faculty member, for example, cope when they are also being asked to support their own children in different grades?

What is abundantly clear is that we need to have a flexible, individual approach to the future blended online, face-to-face educational combination that looks more and more likely to become the new normal. We have opportunities to think about leadership, and development of leaders, in new ways. We also have opportunities to make learning far more adaptive and individualized based on each learner's strengths, but we cannot forget those who have limited access, poor home support, or learning styles that mean they may struggle with the independent learning required in an online environment. So, we must be increasingly flexible and willing to work collaboratively and reflectively to explore different options we may not even have considered yet. We look forward to this collaboration and exploration.

Note

1 See https://en.wikipedia.org/wiki/Dialogue_journal

References

Burton, J. (2000). Learning from teaching practice: A case study approach. *Prospect: A Journal of Australian TESOL, 15*(3), 5–22.

Burton, J. (2005). The importance of teachers writing on TESOL. *TESL-EJ, 9*(2), 1–18. http://tesl-ej.org/ej34/a2.pdf

Burton, J. (2009). Reflective writing – Getting to the heart of teaching and learning. In J. Burton, P. Quirke, C. Reichmann, & J. K. Peyton (Eds.), *Reflective writing: A way to lifelong teacher learning* (pp. 1–11). TESL-EJ, E-Book Edition. http://www.tesl-ej.org/wordpress/books

Burton, J., & Carroll, M. (Eds.). (2001). *Journal writing*. Teachers of English to Speakers of Other Languages.

Burton, J., Quirke, P., Reichmann, C., & Peyton, J. K. (Eds.). (2009). *Reflective writing: A way to lifelong teacher learning*. TESL-EJ, E-Book Edition. http://www.tesl-ej.org/wordpress/books

Louden, W. (1991). *Understanding teaching: Continuity and change in teachers' knowledge*. Teachers College Press.

Quirke, P. (2001). Maximizing student writing and minimizing teacher correction. In J. Burton & M. Carroll (Eds.), *Journal writing* (pp. 11–22). Teachers of English to Speakers of Other Languages.

Sharkey, J., & Johnson, K.E. (Eds.). (2003). *The TESOL Quarterly dialogues: Rethinking issues of language, culture and power*. Teachers of English to Speakers of Other Languages.

Tripp, D. (1993). *Critical incidents in teaching: Developing professional judgement*. Routledge.

Trites, L. (2001) Journals as a self-evaluative, reflective classroom tool: A case study of advanced ESL graduate students. In J. Burton & M. Carrell (Eds.), *Journal writing* (pp. 59–70). Teachers of English to Speakers of Other Languages.

Wells, G., & Chang-Wells, G. L. (1992). *Constructing knowledge together: Classrooms as centers of inquiry and literacy*. Heinemann.

Wenger, E. (1998). *Communities of practice: Learning, meaning, and identity*. Cambridge University Press.

Wenger-Trayner, E., Fenton O'Creevy, M., Hutchinson, S., Kubiak, C., & Wenger-Trayner, B. (2015). *Learning in landscapes of practice: Boundaries, identity, and knowledgeability in practice-based learning*. Routledge.

Index

action research   45, 48, 70, 84, 87, 101, 103, 131
agency   27, 31, 37, 46, 95, 132
appraisal   30, 33, 46
appreciative inquiry   8, 14, 23, 43
assessment   2, 11, 16, 30, 37, 52, 53, 62, 84, 92, 95, 108
authenticity   92, 98
authority   30, 65, 96, 98, 102, 122
autobiographies   4, 16, 108, 120, 132

Bakhtin, M.   12, 67, 73, 81, 90, 100
behavior   6, 24, 31, 36, 44, 50, 93, 94, 110
beliefs   3, 7, 21, 49, 60, 87, 100, 115

case studies   4, 16, 64, 84, 87, 91, 96, 101, 103, 119, 134–135
coaching   1, 2, 9, 10, 18, 64, 104, 117, 118, 121, 123, 129
cognitive   10, 13–14, 20, 21, 66, 104
commitment   2, 27, 30, 31, 33, 40, 69
constructivist   9, 16, 30, 39–40, 45, 46, 49, 90, 98
corporatization   24, 43–44, 131
communities of practice   3, 12, 17, 35, 39, 47, 80, 93, 94, 103, 120, 124, 126, 127, 133
creativity   27, 33, 39, 41, 80, 90, 107, 124, 129, 131
critical reflection   3, 4, 6, 9, 16, 23, 27, 44, 48–49, 52–53, 60, 65, 83, 106, 108, 110, 111, 120, 123
culture   2, 14, 26, 35, 36, 42, 44, 48, 54, 66, 67, 86, 87, 93, 95, 100–103, 111, 112, 120, 126, 135

delegation   34, 35, 113, 114
dialogue journals   4, 11, 15, 49, 50, 60, 61, 70, 107, 108, 111, 119, 131–132, 134
diaries   4, 8, 49, 85, 117, 132
discourse analysis   6, 87, 107
discursive   67–68, 81–82, 96

emotional   18, 37, 41, 44, 75, 113
empowerment   25, 27, 34, 46, 78, 112, 115
engagement   13, 24, 28, 37, 49, 68, 70, 71, 75, 93, 99, 104, 106–111, 113, 117, 118, 122, 123, 128, 133

evaluation   5, 14, 30, 43–46, 48, 51, 87, 92, 106, 118, 119, 122
evidence   2, 6, 25, 27, 28, 44, 49, 64, 84, 108, 113
exploration   6, 8–10, 12, 21, 26, 28, 30, 35, 38, 53, 67, 73, 83, 98, 104, 109, 114, 126–128, 130–132, 134

feedback   2, 6, 29–31, 36, 39–40, 48, 51–55, 58, 63, 78, 81, 85, 96, 97, 106, 110, 128
Freire, P.   5, 12, 65, 67, 79, 82

goals   24, 25, 28, 32, 85–87, 93, 110, 129
guided reflection   4, 22, 31, 37, 48, 50, 52, 60, 62, 76, 100

identity   6, 9–10, 12, 15, 17, 31, 45, 50–51, 65, 67, 71, 72, 77–80, 95, 102–103, 122, 127, 135
inclusion   33, 44, 61, 71, 74, 80, 82, 96, 121, 129
innovation   2, 9, 31, 33, 36, 42, 74, 116, 125
inquiry   1, 8, 12, 14, 20, 42, 47, 53, 68, 83, 84, 90, 92–94, 99, 102, 103, 131
instruction   6, 8, 27, 42, 48, 53–55, 59–62, 75, 108–110, 118, 122, 128, 132
interactive   3, 4, 6, 7, 10, 20, 22–24, 32, 48, 49, 60, 61, 65–68, 72–79, 105–107, 109, 114, 115, 117, 122–124, 128

leadership theories
    adaptive   26, 44, 134
    authentic   35, 44, 92, 98, 100, 111, 122
    balanced scorecard   24, 45
    change   2–3, 12, 14, 23, 26, 34, 40, 43, 44, 49, 50, 64, 109–111, 115, 119, 128, 135
    democratic   24, 25, 36, 47
    distributed   25, 34, 44, 93
    ethical   24, 31, 35, 42, 85–86, 90, 116, 129
    learning-centered   19, 23, 46
    servant   38–39, 44–46
    situational   21–22, 29, 34, 36, 37, 49, 51, 60, 69, 75, 89, 99, 112, 124, 127
    transactional   24, 25, 45
    transformational   21, 24, 25, 42, 45, 120
    values-based   2, 23, 31, 35, 36, 38, 39, 43, 45, 96, 108, 123

INDEX

leadership qualities   9, 27, 122, 127
lifelong learning   13, 21, 101, 122, 133
literacy   13, 15, 16, 47, 65, 67, 68, 70, 72, 73, 80–83, 100–103

meaning   16–17, 20, 38, 53, 61, 76, 77, 90, 96, 110, 131, 133
memoirs   4, 120, 131
mentoring   2, 6, 11, 16, 26, 39, 40, 46, 51–54, 57–64, 93, 111, 120, 129, 132
metaphor   1, 68, 77, 129, 133
methodology   12, 30, 85, 87–90, 92–93, 98, 103
motivation   1, 8, 16, 32–33, 40, 43, 45, 46, 115, 116, 123

patterns of reflective writing
   organization change   5, 6, 12, 25–27, 110, 115
   participant learning   5–7, 25–26, 106, 107, 109, 113
   participant reactions   5–6, 25, 26, 106, 107, 112
   participant use of new knowledge   5, 25, 27, 108, 109, 115
   participation patterns   5, 25–27, 105, 106, 112, 127
   student learning   5–6, 23, 26–29, 37, 55, 79, 111, 116
pedagogy   1, 7, 21, 27–30, 44, 48, 52, 53, 60, 61, 65, 69, 82, 102, 107, 108, 111, 122, 123, 128
perspectives   4, 6, 7, 12, 16, 29, 33, 39, 40, 53, 54, 65, 67–68, 73, 81, 82, 84, 90, 91, 106, 119, 122, 128, 130
portfolios   4, 30, 55, 56, 74, 88, 90, 92, 98, 132
positivity   18, 24, 25, 29, 32, 36, 37, 39, 41–45, 53, 54, 71, 73, 78, 115, 116
power   1, 7–10, 25, 33, 35–36, 44, 50, 80, 96, 98, 99, 104, 105, 117–119, 122, 133, 135

professional development   5, 9–10, 13–15, 17, 19, 25, 27, 28, 30–32, 35, 37, 42, 44, 45, 48, 53, 54, 58–60, 63, 64, 103, 114, 116, 119, 121, 122, 129
purpose   4, 23, 33, 48, 53, 60, 112, 128, 132, 133

qualitative   14, 38, 70, 101–103

reality   2, 16, 71, 107, 122
recognition   1, 32, 33, 38, 39, 45, 49, 115, 121, 125
reflective journals   4, 11, 16, 22, 60, 110, 132
reflective writing typology   6, 7, 29, 30, 130
resistance   31, 46, 50, 63, 102
respect   2, 21, 32–33, 35, 36, 38, 41, 65, 79, 93, 116, 123, 129
responsibility   9, 13, 19, 27, 33, 34, 62, 84, 92, 94, 99, 116, 121, 122, 126, 129

social constructivist   16, 19, 20, 46, 67, 122, 133
strategy   10, 23–25, 29–30, 32, 37, 38, 43, 45, 48, 53–55, 58, 60, 74–77, 84, 95, 96, 116, 124, 127
strengths   1, 11, 21, 24–26, 28, 34, 37, 38, 49, 54, 71, 79, 85, 93, 112

teacher knowledge   20–22, 27, 44, 46, 88, 113, 114
teacher learning   5, 8–10, 13, 49, 88, 96, 99, 105, 111, 117, 119, 124
transparency   30, 61, 92, 115, 127
tutor   1, 23, 25, 30, 31, 34, 35, 48, 118, 123

vision   10, 12, 24–25, 39, 68, 84, 116, 126, 129
voice   10, 11, 27, 44, 65, 67, 70, 72, 73, 96, 98, 102, 107, 119, 122, 126